Montrose J. Moses Jr.
1932.

SIR WALTER SCOTT

SCOTT'S
LADY OF THE LAKE

EDITED BY
JAY EARLE THOMSON

AUTHOR OF "THE LAND OF EVANGELINE,"
"THE LAND OF THE PILGRIMS," ETC.

GOL-
DEN
KEY
SERIES

D. C. HEATH AND COMPANY

BOSTON   NEW YORK   CHICAGO
ATLANTA   SAN FRANCISCO   DALLAS
                 LONDON

Printed in the United States of America

PREFACE

Teachers of English have been preaching for years the need of background in studying literature. A person completely ignorant of the Renaissance, for example, certainly never sees the fine irony of *My Last Duchess;* and no pupil can understand *The Bishop Orders His Tomb* if he has never heard of a bishop and thinks a tomb is a grass-covered mound under a weeping willow.

In *The Lady of the Lake*, the American pupil's first difficulties are a strange locale and unfamiliar history. If these problems are not removed, he never finds out what the tale is all about.

The introductory material in this book is directed at the student, not at the teacher. The author spent four months traveling over the territory in which the story is set; and he has tried to help the pupil by studying the Highlands with modern American eyes. With the idea of background constantly in mind, the author has sketched the story of the Douglas-Stuart feud; for unless a pupil understands that quarrel, he can never understand or enjoy *The Lady of the Lake*.

The notes are brief and are placed at the bottom of the page, because the plot is the thing, and the author's first wish is that the pupil should enjoy a rapid and dramatic tale. By no means should too much emphasis on romantic language and archaic vocabulary be permitted to kill a fine story.

The questions and projects are, of course, directed at the teacher. Many teachers will wish to proceed very much on their own initiative; others will welcome assistance to lighten the teaching load. But both, it is hoped, will profit by the suggestions offered.

JAY EARLE THOMSON

CONTENTS

The Lady of the Lake

Appendix

ILLUSTRATIONS

CHAPTER I

A SUMMER IN THE TROSSACHS

To understand properly the setting of *The Lady of the Lake* let us take a tramp together through the glens and glades of that part of Scotland called the Trossachs. Let us imagine that somehow we have reached "Glenartney's hazel shade." Just there the stag, startled by the "Bloodhound's heavy bay," must have sprung up from "his midnight lair." How chilly it is and how glad we are of the Scotch woolens we have bought for the trip! We toil patiently out of the glen, getting drenched by the dewy foliage and remembering a little ruefully with what ease he cleared the copse and bounded away to the south.

Once out of the glen, we are warmed a bit by the morning sun. We have plenty of time to examine the wild flowers as we tramp through the fields. Off to the north is the barren-topped mountain that so cruelly reëchoed the baying of the hounds to the panting stag, who by this time is gaining the heights of Uam-Var. We pick the different flowers, really meaning to take them home, as we follow the course of the stag southward.

To the west is a beautiful lake, Loch Lubnaig. It looks so far away, and we are so tired and warm that we decide to descend from the "heights of Uam-Var" and find some easier means of travel. In this we feel vindicated in that Mark Twain in his *Tramp Abroad* seemed to tramp very little. On reaching a road, we are soon invited to ride by a hospitable Scot, who is both anxious and willing to tell us tales of Sir Walter and his trips through this region.

We reach Callander on the River Teith. At a comfortable hotel we refresh ourselves. Here Scott is known to have stayed on many occasions. A feeling of animation comes over us as we realize this fact, and in imagination we see him tramping over the country with his notebook and pencil, to procure material and inspiration for *Rob Roy*, *The Legend of Montrose*, and *The Lady of the Lake*. Although Scott stayed in Callander on numerous occasions, he fails to mention it in his story. Literary critics are of the opinion that the word Callander would not rhyme with other words and therefore that town could have no place in our poem. It is an interesting Scotch hamlet at any rate and well worth a visit. It existed as early as 1350, its name in Gaelic meaning *Coill-an tir* or "wood of the land."

From our hotel at Callander we take the principal highway across the Leny River. Along the road are green hedgerows and stone walls, covered with moss and ivy. Highland cattle, ungainly and somewhat scraggly in appearance, feed in the neighboring pastures. Shropshire sheep with their coal-black faces stop nibbling the rich herbage to watch us pass. Presently we pass through the Coilachallan Woods, cross Garchonzie Bridge, and find ourselves on the famous Trossachs road, which in the days of the long ago saw the "tracks of the raider and the 'cattle-lifter.'"

The Trossachs, which means "bristled country" in the ancient Gaelic language, includes that part of Scotland adjacent to Loch Katrine. The authority of custom has stamped its approval on the application of the name "Trossachs" to the section from Callander on the east, to Loch Lomond on the west, and from the stretches of Stirlingshire to the wooded and grassy braes of Balquidder. The district, twenty-five miles in diameter, is studded with treeless mountains and limpid lakes, and abounds in legend and tradition.

The Trossachs road strikes off to the left, but we keep straight on along Bochastle's Ridge. At the hamlet of Kilmahog, a winding road passes to an old fort called Doun Mohr, or "big hill." A large bowlder, probably of glacial origin, attracts many sightseers. From the days of Roman occupation it has been called "Samson's putting stone." An old legend informs us that "Samson one morning was taking exercise on the top of Ben Lomond, and he threw the stone which we see lying where it landed." Grassy mounds, shrub-covered walls, and depressions, filled with débris, give evidence of the Romans who inhabited this place.

Two and one-half miles from Callander we reach the famous Leny Pass. By looking toward the river, we find an opening in the bank with a rough pathway to the riverside. The water for some hundred yards boils down a narrow pass, rockbound on either side. Farther up the stream, the water rushes round a huge bowlder with turbulent fury. Continuing up the Leny, we reach Lake Lubnaig, which we have seen from the "heights of Uam-Var." At the foot of this lake, among stately trees, lies an old cemetery. This was once the site of the Chapel of St. Bride, where

A blithesome rout that morning-tide
Had sought the chapel of Saint Bride.
Her troth Tombea's Mary gave
To Norman, heir of Armandave.

The poem also reminds us that the fleet-footed Angus thrust the Fiery Cross into the hands of Norman at this place, and

Ben Ledi saw the Cross of Fire,
It glanced like lightning up Strath-Ire.

Strath-Ire and St. Fillan in this region are to be recom-
mended as tranquil havens for daydreaming and the
rest that is only to be had among such scenes and in
such a climate. On to the north are the "braes of
Balquidder"

> Let us go, lassie, go, to the braes of Balquidder,
> Where the blaeberries grow 'mang the bonnie Highland heather,
> Where the deer and the roe lightly bounding together
> Sport the lang simmer day on the braes of Balquidder.

immortalized by the poet, Tannahill. It was in this
region of green hills and moorland expanses that Rob
Roy spent his last days and passed to his rest, clad in his
Highland dress with his piper playing the dirge "I'll
Return No More."

Leaving this romantic section, we return to Callander
for our trip through that part of the Trossachs where the
stag hunt ended, and the other places visited by the
chief huntsman, James Fitz-James. Crossing the Teith,
we shall visit a depression of meadowland probably
formed by the glaciers that once passed over this section.
Shaggy long-haired cattle are feeding on the rich fodder
of the pasture. This is Lanrick Mead, the mustering
place of Clan-Alpine. Here the Fiery Cross was thrust
into the hands of the swift runner who was to carry the
word for the rising of the Highlanders.

Here also was the ford that crossed the Teith, the
scene of the combat between Roderick Dhu and Fitz-
James.

> And here his course the Chieftain stayed,
> Threw down his target and his plaid.

From Coilantogle's Ford we ride in a huge motor bus,
which the British call a "charabanc," along the shores
of Loch Vennachar to its source. A meandering stream,
Dhu Abhainn, or Black River, emerges from Loch Ach-

ray and finds its way along grassy shores to Loch Vennachar. Coming over a rise of ground and seeing the cottages of Duncraggan, one half expects to meet the messenger carrying the news of the gathering of the clan. Running down from Loch Katrine, past Loch Achray, Malise was to bear the torch to Duncan of Duncraggan, who was to carry it on. Unknown to him, Duncan lay dead upon his lowly bier; but Angus, the young son, without a moment's hesitation seized the signal and ran on to Lanrick Mead.

Beneath the spreading branches of high trees, we thread our way in the direction of the famous Brigg o' Turk, an arched stone bridge, spanning the Turk, a small stream flowing from the mountains through Glenfinlas Valley. The word *Turk* means "wild boar," and the creek was probably named from the animals that once roamed these fields, the last of which were killed at this place.

A short distance away lies a little hamlet by the same name. Farther up the stony glen, foaming water dashes wildly among broken terraces, throwing itself against weather-worn slabs, and disappearing now and then behind densely covered branches of trees. The adjacent braes with their glowing blossoms of purple heather attract many artists, as well as other travelers.

Off to the northward Ben Ledi towers, broad and bare, above the surrounding country. The region is typical of Highland scenery, wild, uncultivated, beautiful. The scent of bog myrtle, orchises, and bracken fills the air. In the "brown heath and shaggy wood" are rabbits, partridges, and pheasants that, unlike those in America, continue to feed fearlessly when we approach. But where are the red deer that the Knight of Snowdoun used to chase? Some of the residents say that even now they occasionally see them grazing in and about this woodland, but the species has been hunted almost out of existence.

Near Loch Achray the thoroughfare skirts a wooded glen, carpeted with ferns and wild flowers. Among these grows luxuriantly the deep green ground-ivy whose long runners with their clusters of blue-purple blossoms impede the progress of the walker. The fragrant sweet marjoram, the pink-streaked wood sorrel, and the wild geranium with crimson leaves and pink blossoms grow abundantly. Above the plants and flowers rise birch and oak.

Throughout the section we note the accuracy with which the poet has described the lakes, glens, trees, and flowers. In the constant companionship of his dogs, with his notebook and pencil, we can fancy him studying nature as he tramped through the woodlands, fording streams and scaling precipices.

Of the three sister lakes, Achray is the smallest. In Gaelic, Achray means "level field"; hence Loch Achray means "the lake of the level field." It is a tiny lake, not more than a mile long, but its "copsewood gray" and its "pine-trees blue" make a lasting impression on the mind.

> But nearer was the copsewood gray
> That waved and wept on Loch-Achray,
> And mingled with the pine-trees blue
> On the bold cliffs of Ben Venue.

Just beyond the lake is a path with a sign which reads "Through the Old Pass." This was undoubtedly the road of Scott's time. Somewhere in this vicinity Fitz-James lost all trace of the stag which

> dashing down a darksome glen,
> Soon lost to hound and Hunter's ken,
> In the deep Trossachs' wildest nook,
> His solitary refuge took.

After having suffered the loss of his beloved horse, his "gallant gray," he blew his horn to attract his companions. Wandering along the path, the hunter was surprised to see a tiny skiff, bearing a maiden, Ellen, the Lady of the Lake, who was answering what she believed was her father's signal blast. After Fitz-James had related his tales of disappointment and misfortune to the young woman, she invited him to the island, the home of Sir Roderick, an outlaw and enemy of the crown.

At the first glimpse of Loch Katrine, we are reminded of a "burnished sheet of living gold." The pier, hemmed in by furrowed hills and dense copsewood, lies near the end of the Trossachs road. A Scotch Highlander, dressed after the custom of his people, stands near the wharf, playing on his bagpipe. A little boy, similarly dressed, who is probably the son of the musician, appears at the conclusion of the recital, doffs his cap, and proceeds to collect a few coins from the tourists.

The *Sir Walter Scott*, a long white steamboat, lies at the dock waiting to take us for a sail on the deep blue waters of Loch Katrine. A bookseller is reaping a large harvest disposing of copies of *The Lady of the Lake* to those who want to read the story in its actual setting.

Above the wharf looms a craggy height, known as "Sir Roderick's Watch Tower." Silhouetted against gray Ben Venue, this tree-covered cliff stands out sharply beside the silvery waters of the lake. As we see it basking in the sunlight of midday, we recall how it served Sir Roderick and his guards as a sentinel post from which they could watch the approach of the enemy.

A meandering path conducts the traveler through dense copsewood, beneath shaggy trees and among glacial bowlders to the top of the watch tower. The summit, clothed with a cluster of evergreens and oaks, and richly covered with purple heather, has many memories for us. Aged pines interspersed among the white birches and luxuriant wild flowers fill the air with fragrance. The notes of hidden song birds echo among the rocks and rills.

From the peak of this glacial formation a panorama of unusual interest spreads out in all directions. Lochs Achray and Vennachar lie like pools of liquid silver, among the long, green stretches of luxuriant herbage. Above them towers cloud-capped Ben Venue, whose treeless, wind-swept sides extend to the water's edge. A little to the right we behold a rocky amphitheater, Goblin's Cave, to which Ellen and her father retreated from Sir Roderick's stronghold. Beyond the Coir-nan-Uriskin extends a furrowed stretch called Beala-nam-bo, "the pass of the cattle," where, in the old days, the cattle, captured in raids or forays on the Lowlanders, were driven to some secret hiding place.

The shimmering waters of Loch Katrine, nestled at the base, take their way westward between rugged grass-covered heights, while the relentless blue of the sky gives the landscape a tinge of pearly gray. In the foreground we see a small island, shaped like a pyramid, crowned with trees,

> Where for retreat in dangerous hour
> Some chief had framed a rustic bower.

From the pier a path, the continuation of the Trossachs road, on which vehicles are forbidden, winds along the irregular shore of Loch Katrine for several miles. Where is the "silver strand" that Scott visited and described? The city of Glasgow now uses Loch Katrine as a source of water supply. To make the lake a more satisfactory reservoir, the level of the water has been raised, and the "silver strand" is now completely submerged. Walking along the path, we see in imagination the tiny skiff bearing James Fitz-James and Ellen across the lake to the isle.

Ellen's Isle, the picturesque gem of the Trossachs, lies about seventy-five yards from the white pebbly beach. Covered with a sturdy growth of silvery birch, oak, willows, and evergreens, the island is beautiful in the sunlight. Now and then a lonesome pine, high and straight, rises above its neighbors. In front of the glacial rocks that generations ago sheltered Sir Roderick and his clan, grow patches of purple heather. In the autumn the heather blossoms change the soft mass of herbage to violet or lavender.

On the shore where we are standing, a sparkling brook dashes down the mountainside, splashes against projecting rocks, and continues its winding course until its waters join those of Loch Katrine. At this spot, according to tradition, came Ellen in response to the blast of the horn.

Behind us looms Ben Aan whose velvety green summit seems to pierce the yellow-tinted clouds. This bold mountain frowns upon the scene, and looks across the lake to Ben Venue with steep sides that have been furrowed and wrinkled by the elements. Near Goblin's Cave, we note a swift mountain torrent rushing madly down the mountainside, creating a streak of white mist and foam.

Owing to the inconvenience of visiting the island, few travelers make the attempt to see its beauties. A lusty mountaineer of the Highlands consented to row us across the "narrow inlet, still and deep," to Ellen's Isle. Our visit strengthened our admiration for the accuracy of Scott's descriptions.

By his accuracy in *The Lady of the Lake*, Scott greatly endeared himself to the natives of this section. After reading the description of Sir Roderick's den, they erected a hut and furnished it with relics, pictures, and trophies of the chase. Only a group of moss-covered

bowlders now marks the spot, however, for in 1837 it
caught fire and burned.

Looking up the lake toward Glengyle, one can almost
see

> slow enlarging on the view,
> Four mann'd and masted barges grew,
> And, bearing downwards from Glengyle,
> Steer'd full upon the lonely isle. . . .

It was the gathering of the clan to which Ellen be-
longed —

> Ever, as on they bore, more loud
> And louder rung the pibroch proud.
> . . . .
> "Roderick Vich Alpine, ho! iro!"

As they came nearer, the words of the boat song became
distinguishable,

> Hail to the Chief who in triumph advances!

Ellen came reluctantly to greet her kinsmen, knowing
too well that her bold cousin sought her hand in marriage
while her heart had long since been given to another —
Malcolm Graeme. To a Highlander in the old days, the
love of his clan surpassed all other loves, and Sir Roderick
putting aside his disappointment and jealousy went on
about his business — to gather his kinsmen for war.

Beyond the Trossachs in the crimson west the sun is
sinking beneath golden-tinted clouds. Soft breezes from
the lakes stir the rustling leaves. The lengthening of
the shadows on the braes indicates the approach of
evening. A gray mist has settled about the tops of the
mountains, while the ever-changing clouds in the back-
ground seem to magnify them.

CHAPTER II

AT STIRLING

THE romance and history of Stirling Castle hold more than a common interest for travelers. James V, the Fitz-James of the poem, was crowned king at the age of one year in the castle; on Abbey Craig stands the monument to Wallace, the defender of Scotch freedom and independence; at Bannockburn lie the fields where Bruce defeated the British and won his crown; and about the little town lie the green plains, winding streams, and hills that played so important a part in the days of chivalry.

Three miles south of Stirling on a little tributary of the Forth lies the village of Bannockburn. Here with thirty thousand Scots, Robert Bruce defeated the English king, Edward II, who had at his command one hundred thousand trained warriors. Near the scene of battle lies the "Bore Stone," the hilltop on which the Scotch leader is said to have "fixed his standard" during the battle. Near the center of the field today stands a flagstaff one hundred twenty feet high from which flies the Union Jack.

Mac Culloch in 1824, over one hundred years ago, described Stirling as follows: "But it is not of Stirling of which I need to speak, the glory of Scotland; for who does not know its noble rock, rising like a monarch of the landscape, its majestic and picturesque towers, its amphitheater of mountain, and the windings of its marvelous river; and who, that has once seen the sun descending here in all the blaze of its beauty beyond the blue hills of the west, can ever forget the plains of Stirling, the endless charm of the wonderful scene, the wealth, the splendor, the variety, the majesty of all which here lies between earth and heaven?"

Like the castle at Edinburgh, the one at Stirling occupies a towering cliff. From its battlements guides point out seven battlefields, where Scottish power and destiny swayed in the balance. Its towers, walls, turrets, and battlements are signs of its great age. Around its gray sides once glistened long English pikes, held in the hands of armored soldiers; on the steep and overhanging sides, men with bows and battle-axes fought for possession of the stronghold; around its massive walls are buried dauntless soldiers of both armies who sacrificed their lives for their kings. On the broad plains before the castle, in mediæval days, festivals and tournaments took place.

From the base of the cliff, we follow the road to the Lady's Rock, the place where the women sat and witnessed the jousting and the less noble contests. In robes of green and gray Ben Lomond, Ben Voirlich, and Ben Ledi rise above the tree-covered plains. In the opposite direction we see the Union Jack flying above the battlefield at Bannockburn. Below us is the famous King's Knot, where the Scottish nobility met for their tourneys. According to our poet, the Douglas proved his strength at this spot.

> The Douglas rent an earth-fast stone
> From its deep bed, then heaved it high,
> And sent the fragment through the sky,
> A rood beyond the farthest mark;
> And still in Stirling's royal park,
> The grey-hair'd sires, who know the past,
> To strangers point the Douglas cast,
> And moralise on the decay
> Of Scottish strength in modern day.

As with most castles, a moat, now empty of water, surrounds this ancient stronghold. To enter the fortress, we cross the drawbridge as did the occupants centuries ago. There are so many chambers, halls, dungeons, promenades, and courts, that a description of them all would require a volume instead of a few paragraphs. Therefore we shall acquaint ourselves with a few of the most interesting places, so that we may have a better understanding of the Knight of Snowdoun and his castle.

Beyond the drawbridge and beneath a stone archway, we note the Inner Ditch, the Overport Battery, Queen Anne's Battery, and the French Battery, which was erected in 1559 when Mary of Guise, the queen of our hero, James Fitz-James, was trying to defend the interests of her little orphaned daughter. There is the palace which was built during the reigns of James IV and our hero, James V. This magnificent and spacious building had only a brief existence, for it was practically demolished by artillery fire a hundred years later. Passing through long corridors, we come to the Lion's Den, where the Stuart kings, like all kings of the time, kept lions in imitation of Nero at Rome.

The old armory is quite similar to the armories at the Tower of London, Warwick Castle, Edinburgh Castle, and Sir Walter Scott's home at Abbotsford. Specimens of guns, bows, spears, battle-axes, helmets, armor, and other weapons used in early warfare are to be found in this chamber. These are carefully arranged to show the evolution of methods and materials used in killing human beings. These primitive yet priceless relics of brutal and savage warfare remind us of the days when the lords and noblemen practiced the doctrine,

> He shall take who has the power,
> And he shall keep who can.

Wandering about the fortress, now used by the government as barracks for soldiers, we enter the Douglas room,

which is said to be the guard room, mentioned by Scott
in the sixth canto. The room contains numerous arti-
cles of furniture that were used by the House of Douglas.
Many paintings, carefully preserved, adorn the walls.
In an adjacent room there is a window that contains the
Douglas coat of arms.

Before leaving the historic landmark, we must pay a
brief visit to the Douglas Garden, where members of the
Douglas family were accustomed to take their leisure.
Old Stirling Bridge, a structure of four graceful arches
built in 1410, the Gowan Hills, the Abbey Craig with
Wallace's Monument, Cambuskenneth Abbey, the wind-
ings of the Forth, and the towering peaks of the Gram-
pians stand out prominently on the landscape and make
charming pictures. Such a view can be seen only from
this garden.

Our trip to Stirling, the key to the Highlands, is not
complete without paying a visit to the Abbey Craig with
its stately Wallace Monument. This tower, erected in
1869, commemorates the victory of the Scots over the
English at Stirlingbridge in 1297. Because of Sir William
Wallace's fierce attacks on the invading English, who
were constantly trying to conquer Scotland, he became
an outlaw. Raising a large force of archers and spear-
men, he succeeded in expelling the English from Aber-
deen and adjacent places. At the youthful age of
twenty-three he led the Scotch army that triumphed
over the English at Stirling.

A curved path, lined with dark-green shrubs and fra-
grant flowers, leads to the monument, which rises two
hundred twenty feet above the ground. In the monu-
ment we see the "hall of heroes," which contains the
busts of Robert the Bruce, Robert Burns, John Knox,
Sir Walter Scott, and about a dozen other famous Scots.
The reception hall is decorated with mementos of the

THE WILLIAM WALLACE MONUMENT

The English kings tried for centuries to conquer their northern neighbors. The Scots are still proud of their heroes, who again and again repelled the invaders. The two great names are Wallace, who was finally captured and executed, and Robert Bruce, who defeated Edward II at Bannockburn. Photo by Ewing Galloway.

past — the shining armor, sharp spears, Wallace's sword, and many a curious relic of the warlike past; and the stained glass windows depict early chapters of Scotland's stormy history.

A climb of exactly two hundred forty-six steps brings us to the top. A view similar to the one from the Douglas Garden spreads out before us. Below, Stirling Castle, age-worn and gloomy, seems calm and peaceful in the afternoon sunlight. The gorgeous sunset, the rustling of the leaves, and the babbling waters of the near-by Forth help us to imagine the aged minstrel, Allan-bane, playing on his ancient harp and chanting words of inspiration.

CHAPTER III

MINE OWN ROMANTIC TOWN — EDINBURGH

EDINBURGH has been called the "Athens of the North." Those of us who have visited the Greek and Scottish capital cities can see a striking similarity between them. An adjacent sea, neighboring mountains, ancient and modern avenues, universities, libraries, museums, observatories, and terraced gardens are found in both cities. In Athens we look with wonder upon the Acropolis; in Edinburgh we note a similar eminence in the heart of the city — Castle Rock. Like the city of Pericles, Edinburgh has produced scholars, men of letters, and scientists.

Perhaps the best description of Edinburgh may be found in the writings of Sir Walter Scott. He stood near Salisbury Crag overlooking the city when he wrote: "The prospect in its general outline commands a close-built, high-piled city stretching itself out beneath in a form which, to a romantic imagination, may be supposed

PRINCES STREET, EDINBURGH

On the cliff in the background is Edinburgh Castle, a little town in itself — so impregnable that it was never captured in the old days except by treachery. The Sir Walter Scott monument is at the right. Courtesy of the London and Northeastern Railway. Copyright by A. N. Robinson.

to resemble that of a dragon, now a noble arm of the sea, with its rocks, isles, distant shores, and boundary of mountain; and now a fair fertile country varied with hill, dale, and rock, and skirted by the picturesque ridge of the Pentland Hills. When a piece of scenery so beautiful, so varied — so exciting by its intricacy, and yet so sublime — is lighted by the tints of morning or of evening, and displays all the variety of shadowy depth exchanged with poetical brilliancy, which gives character even to the torrent of landscape, the effect approaches near to enchantment."

The weather at Edinburgh is typical of some of the coastal cities of Great Britain. From the waters of the neighboring North Sea, cold fogs are ushered in by sea breezes and often cover the city with a blanket of white mist. Unexpected showers, variable winds, and changes of temperature vex the tourist, but the inhabitants are so acclimated that they do not complain of the inconsistencies of the weather. The city is actually as far north as Labrador, and snows from the Highlands come early in the autumn and usually remain until late in the spring. Regardless of the climatic conditions, the beauty, traditions, and romance of Edinburgh lure us to remain indefinitely.

No street in the world is more picturesque and magnificent than Edinburgh's most famous thoroughfare — Princes Street. On the north side are quaint shops, old-fashioned hotels, and cozy dwellings; on the opposite side are monuments, terraced gardens studded with flowers of many colors, tall trees, and long stretches of velvety green grass. On a steep cliff overlooking the street towers Edinburgh Castle.

There are monuments to David Livingston, Adam Black, "Christopher North," Allan Ramsay, Dr. Thomas Guthrie, and Sir James Y. Simpson. Above them rises the graceful Gothic monument erected to the memory of Sir Walter Scott, the author of *The Lady of the Lake*. From early in the morning until late at night, travelers visit these shrines; for the Scots, like every other people, are proud of their great men and certainly they have had their share.

Throughout the world we find imposing monuments erected to the memory of famous statesmen, soldiers, and scientists. But nowhere do we find a memorial like the one that has been erected for Sir Walter Scott. Composed of red sandstone, and approximately two hundred feet high, the Gothic structure with its spires, pinnacles, arches, and turrets, stands as a silent testimony not only of Scotland's but of the world's love and admiration for this distinguished man. Beneath this great canopy is a marble statue of the poet-novelist.

A close view of the memorial reveals, in the shadows of its niches, figures representing many principal characters in Scott's poems and novels. They seem so natural and lifelike to us that we are inclined to think the designer must have known the originals.

We ascend the dark, winding stairways to the top of the shaft. After a long and tedious climb we arrive at the topmost spire. With a dizzy depth below us and the sky above mottled with dark, heavy clouds, a panorama is spread out before our vision. From east to west, from the gray north to the high hills of the south lies the country that Scott loved and celebrated in his writings. Below us, Princes Street stretches in one long silvery line. Only a few blocks away are the famous Assembly Rooms on George Street, where Scott, before a company of friends, admitted the authorship of the Waverley Novels.

Softly silhouetted against the grayish-white mists of the North Sea stands the celebrated Forth Bridge, a triumph in modern engineering skill and perseverance.

It is unfortunately too far away for us to appreciate its symmetry of design and its gigantic massiveness. With the Swiss zigzag roads and our own Panama Canal, this bridge ranks as one of the greatest engineering feats of the age.

Beyond the red and gray-tiled roofs we see dimly in the misty north the region of the Trossachs, the scene of *The Lady of the Lake*. In the opposite direction, among the rolling hills, lies Abbotsford, where Scott spent his last days. Away at the foot of Salisbury Crag we can see the pointed towers of Holyrood Palace, once the home of Mary, Queen of Scots. If those walls could speak, they would thrill us with tales of treachery, strife, and murder. To the west of us we see the wind-swept rock that supports Edinburgh Castle. The courtyards and the grotesque battlements are silent reminders of the struggles that have taken place there.

Through our travels in the Alps, Apennines, Black Forest, and along the mountains overlooking the Rhine and the Neckar, we were impressed by the fact that so many of the castles, (former scenes of happiness and contentment, misery and sorrow) lay in ruins. Fortunately, the ancient castle at Edinburgh, probably begun before the days of the Roman conquest of Britain, has not shared the same fate. This relic of mediæval times that sheltered the executioner, concealed the assassin, and heard the sighs of prisoners, still broods over the landscape; and the Highland guards in kilts still turn out to parade there to the skirl of the bagpipes.

To understand and appreciate Scott, travelers from many lands visit his homes and haunts. Just a glimpse of these places brings us into closer contact with the poet and novelist. To saunter along Scott's streets, to linger at his famous bookstores, to look upon the antique shops and dwellings, which have not changed much in the past century, to gaze upon the green terraces, dotted with plants and fragrant flowers gives the traveler a kind of intimacy with him.

Walking past time-honored dwellings, we find our way from the monument to 8 Chambers Street. A weather-worn tablet informs us that the Scottish man of letters was born here. While he was a small child, this house was torn down to provide space for a portion of the University of Edinburgh. The family then moved to 25 George Square, a modest dwelling, near the center of the fashionable residential section of Edinburgh.

Scott writes that he attended school in a "small cottage-like building with a red-tiled roof, in Hamilton's Entry, off Bristol Street." Later he attended high school in a building which is now a portion of the City Hospital at the foot of Infirmary Street. Old residents affirm that the exterior of the structure has not changed much with the passing decades.

When Scott married Charlotte Margaret Charpentier on Christmas Eve, 1797, he took his bride to 108 George Street. Later they occupied the residence at 19 South Castle Street but soon moved to 39 Castle Street, where they settled down for a quarter of a century. In speaking of "dear old 39," Scott remarked that it had sheltered him from the prime of his life to its decline.

In following Scott through his "romantic town," we must saunter along many of the avenues, alleys, and parks. On Princes Street Scott often strolled, admiring the well-kept lawns and terraces and pausing to greet his many friends. As he limped about the Old or New Town, people from all walks of life grasped the opportunity to shake the hand of their friend and fellow-townsman.

In fancy we accompany him as he passes to the ivy-covered cemetery where he has had a grey slab placed over the grave of "Helen Walker," the humble individual who practiced in real life the virtues with which fiction has invested the imaginary character of "Jeanie Deans." We may also see him entering a stone building at 10 St. Johns Street, where he discussed the Waverley Novels with his friend and publisher, James Ballantyne. Or we may walk with him into the library at 10 Princes Street, where he spent many hours reading.

As we leave Edinburgh with its scenic grandeur and noble mountains we realize what an indelible impression it has made upon our minds. It was through his novels and his poems, like *The Lady of the Lake*, that the master romanticist not only revealed to the world the beauty and charm of this section of Scotland, but in doing so endeared himself to the hearts of English-speaking people for years to come.

CHAPTER IV

A VISIT TO SCOTT'S COUNTRYSIDE

WHEN Washington Irving visited Scott, Abbotsford was being built, but was still largely a dream of the poet. Scott wanted to live like a great Scottish nobleman of an earlier day in a splendid house, surrounded by his family and his friends, welcoming everybody to his door with generous hospitality. But unwise investments in a publishing house left him saddled with enormous debts just at the time Abbotsford was completed. Visiting this great house and the poet's final resting place at Dryburgh Abbey has attracted English, Scots, and Americans for a hundred years.

It was early in the morning of a midsummer's day when we left our hotel at Galashiels for a journey on foot to Scott's countryside at Abbotsford. Every hill and dale was a reminder of the Scottish bard. The sun stood

ABBOTSFORD

Sir Walter Scott built his house when it was very much the fashion to be interested in the romantic past. That is why he added so many turrets and pinnacles. Photo by Ewing Galloway.

high above us as we emerged from beneath a green
canopy of elms near the poet's mansion. On our right a
rather long mountain frowned on the landscape; on
the left the river Tweed glided along pebbly shores that
glistened in the sunlight. The fields, dotted with wild
flowers of rich colors, the songs of the birds, and the gen-
tle winds, carrying the sweet aroma of the bog myrtle
added charm to the place.

Wandering along the road where the poet used to
stroll and meditate, we began to think we had probably
passed the wicket gate, the entrance to Abbotsford, for
no mansion that resembled the photographs of the fa-
mous country home had been visible. Then, just ahead,
we noticed twoscore people leaving a charabanc, and
another large group coming from an enclosure. At last
we had arrived at our destination. The flower garden
and a portion of the magnificent home were now clearly
in view. The house and grounds were so walled in by
nature that an unobserving person might pass by with-
out seeing them.

Serenaded by the song of a lark and the cooing of
doves, we passed through the entrance. A deep, per-
vading peace dominated the grounds that were as vel-
vety and immaculate as a costly Persian rug. The flower
garden, the trees, and the stately mansion reflected the
ambition and kindly personality of the bard. Aside from
the almost noiseless footsteps of a few visitors and the
song of the birds, there was no sound but the gliding
waters of the Tweed. We tried to visualize Scott and
Irving as more than a century ago they ambled over the
grounds, discussing the books, poems, and the romantic
history they both loved.

The major portion of the house consists of blue whin-
stone, with the doorways and windows of sandstone. In
building it, Scott did not confine himself to any particu-

lar style of architecture. Although the structure is odd
and somewhat grotesque, it does not seem unbecoming
nor ridiculous; for its castellated turrets, irregular win-
dows, Gothic stonework, and other unusual features give
it real charm and dignity.

Scott wanted to make Abbotsford unique among the
homes of his friends. From various places he procured
stones which contained inscriptions and figures, and these
he placed in the walls of his house regardless of any plan.
Somebody gave him an old door that had once closed
the portals of the Tolbooth at Edinburgh. Naturally,
Scott wanted to use this relic somewhere in his building.
Today we find this door carefully cemented into one of
the walls, but not as an entrance. Above it there is this
inscription: "The Lord of armies is my protector;
blessit ar thay that trust in the Lord. 1575." At the
right of one of the entrances there stands a marble effigy
of Scott's favorite dog, Maida, beneath which, in Latin,
the poet had inscribed a tribute to his companion.

A narrow lane through the flower garden and court,
lined with dark-green shrubs, leads to the entrance where
guides are stationed, who for a shilling conduct people
through the house. Our dignified guide was dressed
somewhat after the fashion of the days of Scott. His
black skullcap, long black flowing frock, and highly pol-
ished boots would have enabled him to pass for a pro-
fessional pall bearer.

The reception hall contained many interesting relics
of the early days. The roof of the room was arched, the
walls were oak-paneled, and the floor was mosaic. Our
attention was directed to two complete suits of highly
polished armor, once probably used by some huge
fighters. One of these steel suits stood over six feet high
and held a helmet thirty-one inches in circumference.
Our guide drew a smile from members of the party

when he said: "The man who wore this had a 'swelled head.'" Accompanying this armored suit was a huge sword; the blade was six feet seven inches long and the handle was twenty inches.

From the hall our party followed the guide into the most interesting and fascinating room in the building — the study of Sir Walter Scott. The poet's table and desk, which were made from portions of the wood of the ships of the Spanish Armada, his comfortable armchair, shelves of books, and numerous portraits remain as they were in his time. In this room Sir Walter wrote many of his poems and ballads and several of his novels. In the adjacent tower room there were other curios, such as Sir Walter's walking stick, forestry implements, and other personal belongings. In a glass case were the drab trousers, striped vest, blue coat, and high white hat that he wore during his last days.

To many of us the library, containing approximately twenty thousand volumes, was almost as interesting as Sir Walter's study. The volumes in their original bindings stood on the shelves, untouched since the days the poet studied them. The guide pointed out Montfaucon's *Antiquities*, which was presented by King George IV. The priceless ebony writing desk, the gift of George III, the carved elbow chairs, presented by the Pope, and other relics are silent reminders of Scott's popularity with the great men of his day.

To visit the armory it was necessary to pass through the well-kept drawing-room which contained old portraits, drawings by Turner, and a set of ebony chairs, the gift of King George IV. The armory is a narrow, low-arched, dimly lighted room which contains countless articles collected by Scott. Among the relics were a musket used by the famous outlaw, Rob Roy, which bears his initials, R. M. C.; polished Roman spears;

matchlocks; the hunting flask of King James VI; Napoleon's pistols, found in his carriage after his capture and arrest at Waterloo; and scores of ancient weapons and devices used in torturing unfortunate prisoners. After we had looked upon these interesting guns and old curios, the guide described a device that was common at the time. It was placed just above the exit door. In the olden days women were often accused of talking too freely. This steel mechanism, when placed in a proper position, held a woman's mouth shut and so kept her from talking. A cruel way to punish unfortunate victims! But the guide assured us that the device did not prevent the women from talking with their fingers in the mute language.

From Abbotsford we go to Dryburgh Abbey, where the body of our poet lies among the scenes he loved and admired. To visit this charming place, we shall travel along Scott's favorite roads and lanes and look upon the scenes he has so beautifully described.

History informs us that Dryburgh Abbey was founded in 1150 upon the ground where the Druids used to worship in the early days of Britain. In 1322, King Edward II of England practically destroyed the building by fire. Although Robert I restored the abbey, it was again demolished by an English invasion in 1545. The ruins changed ownership several times, but finally the Halliburtons of Mertoun, Walter Scott's ancestors, became the owners.

Despite the fact that the hand of man and the elements have devastated the major portion of the abbey, evidences of its former magnificence may still be seen. The west entrance has a Norman door containing considerable ornamental molding. One finds in the ruins English, Gothic, and Roman styles of architecture. In olden days people built their churches when they had the

money; and if they were poor, years passed before com-
pletion. That is why they had time to change their
minds so often and to build one building in several
styles.

The most interesting part of the abbey is the tomb of
Sir Walter Scott, who was buried in 1832 beside his wife,
who had died a few years before. Also in this same aisle
of the transept lie the remains of their son Lieutenant-
Colonel Walter Scott, who died at sea, and John
Gibson Lockhart, Scott's son-in-law, biographer, and
friend.

The simple unadorned tomb stands among the humble
ruins of Dryburgh Abbey. Around it lie fallen stones,
moss-covered brick, broken masonry, and gray columns.
Grouped about it is a cluster of Scotch spruces which ap-
pear to be standing guard. Their lustrous green seems
symbolical of the fact that the novels and poems of the
famous bard will continue to live.

A velvety rug of grass covers the tiled floor. A serene
peace pervades the ruined edifice. Soft breezes stir the
rustling leaves; the hushed song of birds comes from the
fallen walls; and near-by tranquilly flows

> Tweed's silver streams
> Glittering in the sunny beams.

CHAPTER V

MEDIÆVAL MINSTRELSY

THE opening stanzas of *The Lady of the Lake* are an
invocation to the harp, emblematic of ancient
Scottish minstrelsy. At the end of the last canto of the
poem, the poet takes leave of the harp which he here in-
vokes. Throughout the poem we find several allusions to

minstrels and minstrelsy. At one time the harp was recognized officially as the national instrument of Scotland. A brief review of minstrelsy during the Middle Ages will help us to understand the poem.

The word minstrel is derived from the French *menestrel*, or *menestral*, which means a singer or player of musical instruments. Minstrelsy was a profession to which people, skilled in the arts of music and poetry, belonged. They traveled over the country chanting songs or poems, accompanied by some kind of instrument, usually a harp. In our mediæval literature we read a great deal about these minstrels and the way in which they went from city to city entertaining the populace. With the decline of chivalry, however, the minstrels decreased in numbers and importance.

In biblical history we find an account of minstrelsy among the Children of Israel. Musical instruments were used at ceremonies, festivals, and church services. In Numbers x, 9 we read: "If ye go to war then shall ye blow an alarm with silver trumpets." In another biblical account we learn that seven priests blew their trumpets of ram's horns when Joshua besieged Jericho. Isaiah informs us that at feasts the musicians used the harp, viol, taboret, and pipe. Other instruments used in biblical times were the timbrel, psaltery, cornet, cymbal, bagpipes, bells, and lyre. In reciting their poetry the Israelites were usually accompanied by harps.

As far as we know the custom of minstrelsy accompanied the tides of civilization that swept westward. Rough sketches, old tapestries, copper coins, and time-worn manuscripts found in the monasteries indicate that minstrelsy was a recognized art. People of all the different social classes enjoyed it. Kings employed minstrels in their castles. In *The Domesday Book*, which was planned by William the Conqueror and is now carefully preserved in London, there is mention of a king's minstrel who owned property in Gloucestershire.

In the British Museum in London there are numerous pictures which portray the minstrels of the mediæval days. One shows a royal family at a table covered with costly silk. As the servants bring in the food, two minstrels stand in the corner of the room playing the violin, while another plays the cittern. Other pictures reveal harpers who are chanting poems, accompanying themselves on their instruments.

Throughout England and Scotland the nobility were accustomed to employ one or more minstrels who played on their instruments or sang at different times. In the old castles there were music chambers and chapels where the owners went to hear music or to worship. It was customary for the minstrels to take an active part in all social functions and also in divine meetings. We find them in the monasteries, at weddings, funerals, battles, and athletic events. Obviously, they played an important part in the life of the country during the Middle Ages.

All through these two kingdoms people from the countryside attended the frequent tournaments in great numbers. At these gatherings there were always many minstrels, for it was believed that music inspired both men and horses to attack their opponents with greater strength and fortitude.

In many places in the poem Sir Walter speaks of "errant minstrels." In addition to the minstrels attached to the kings, noblemen, abbots, and bishops, there were those called "errant minstrels," who traveled from one end of the land to the other. From monastery to cathedral, from palace to castle, from the homes of the poor to those of the rich, they wandered playing their instruments and chanting verses. Everywhere people greeted

A SCOTCH PIPER

Every clan had its own *tartan;* that is, a certain design in woolen cloth for kilt and cape, as shown in the picture. Scots by the name of Cameron, Gordon, and Campbell are proud to this day to wear their traditional colors. The great purse on the front of the kilt is called a *sporran*, and was used for food more often than for money. Photo by Brown Brothers.

them courteously and enthusiastically and listened to
their inspiring strains.

The cold wintry blasts and the almost impassable
highways, covered with snow and ice, worked great
hardships on these wandering musicians. Patiently they
waited for the return of the summer birds from the south-
land and the appearance of the spring flowers. Then
they left their solitary abodes and responded to the lure
of the hedgerows and the adventures that awaited them
in the hills and plains. As they journeyed on their way
in the early days of spring, they were greeted by brother
minstrels, knights, pilgrims, and peasants. What re-
joicing there was on the part of the villagers and country
folk! The inhabitants had also spent a lonely winter,
and the presence of the minstrels announced the coming
of spring. One of the songs the minstrels sang in spring
time has been preserved:

> Merry is the ente of May;
> The fowles maketh merry play;
> The time is hot, and long the day.
> The joyful nightingale singeth,
> In the grene mede flowers springeth.

In the first stanza of the second canto of *The Lady of
the Lake*, we read:

> And sweetly o'er the lake was heard thy strain,
> Mix'd with the sounding harp, O white-hair'd Allan-bane!

In this second canto we become acquainted with Allan-
bane, the old harper and minstrel, faithful follower of
the Douglas family. Just as the flashes of red appeared
above the horizon, the seer sat on the pebbly beach with
Ellen and sang while the Knight of Snowdoun rowed in a
skiff across the bay to the opposite shore. Ellen requested
the minstrel to sing praises of her lover, Malcolm, but
instead of happy strains, his song was sad.

Through the poem minstrelsy plays an important part. For example, in the fourth canto Allan-bane endeavors through song to cheer and comfort Ellen while her father is absent on an unknown mission. He also helps her search for the Douglas in Stirling Castle. Later Allan-bane sits in the cell with Roderick Dhu, singing to him of the great battle of Beal' an Duine. In this case, however, the battle song is blended at last into a death dirge; for while Allan-bane is still singing, Sir Roderick dies.

CHAPTER VI

WHO'S WHO AMONG THE PRINCIPAL CHARACTERS

FOR a long time there had been in the Kingdom of Scotland two distinct classes of people; the Highlanders and the Lowlanders. Both factions were made up of independent, lawless people who frequently would not obey the laws of their king unless they were compelled to. Consequently, there was almost a continuous warfare in the Scottish Kingdom.

The Highlanders occupied the mountainous section of Scotland; the Lowlanders held land mostly in the south and west. In speech, manners, customs, and modes of warfare they were unlike each other. The Highlanders were a dark-complexioned Celtic people, like the Irish and Welsh. The Lowlanders were tall, fair, and inclined to be red-haired, more like the English. They resembled each other, however, in being divided into clans or tribes whose chieftains they obeyed and respected more than they did the king. Between these two peoples there was a continuous quarrel. Men of one group would make raids into the territory of the other, plundering and murdering as they went.

The kings of Scotland tried very hard to put down these fighting chieftains. They built roads into the inaccessible mountains and forests, forbade ordinary people to carry firearms, and attempted to enforce law and order. Gradually this policy produced a more tolerant feeling between the Highlanders and Lowlanders. Instead of plundering and fighting, the people began to settle down to agricultural pursuits and the foundation for a strong and united people was laid.

JAMES FITZ-JAMES

The James Fitz-James of the poem is none other than James V, of Scotland, son of James IV of Scotland and Margaret, the sister of King Henry VIII of England. At the Battle of Flodden James IV lost his life. Though the heir to the throne was less than two years old, he became king, while his mother assumed the regency of the kingdom. This position she might have held indefinitely, for she was much loved, had it not been for an unfortunate move on her part which cost her her popularity with her subjects.

Margaret, after her husband's death, had married the Earl of Angus, of the great Douglas family. Like her brother Henry VIII of England, who tired of his wives, she seemed to tire of her husbands. She obtained a divorce from Angus and married a young man of inferior rank. Through this act she lost her influence, while her former husband, Angus, rose in power. He obtained possession of the person of the young king and, conducting everything in his name became the real regent of the kingdom. Things went well for a while until old hatreds and jealousies arose. It was said that the Douglas showed great partiality to his own kinsmen, and that justice itself was sadly perverted.

No sooner had James entered young manhood than he began to chafe under the restraining hand of the Douglas. Twice he attempted to escape from the guards who kept a continuous watch over him, but to no avail. The third time he made his plans more carefully. He persuaded his mother, Queen Margaret, to turn over Stirling Castle to him, which he put in charge of a governor whom he could trust. Then, one day, under the pretense of hunting he fled to Stirling Castle. The gates were opened to receive him and closed upon his pursuers. From this stronghold he gathered about him friendly noblemen and announced his intention to rule Scotland himself. He denounced all of the house of Douglas and sent them into exile. Their goods were confiscated, and none by that name was permitted to own land in Scotland.

This resolution of the king was carried out even under circumstances when it seemed cruel and unnecessary. There is a story which tells of old Archibald Douglas of Kilspindie, who had been a great favorite of the boy king. Finding himself homesick and unhappy in his exile and feeling that, since he was so old, the king would not distrust him nor fear to have him back in Scotland, he returned and begged the king's mercy. He ran along beside the mounted king until he found himself lying on the ground exhausted outside the gates of Stirling. The king, although he knew him and wished to greet his old friend, would not bend from his decision. The servants in the castle dared not even grant the old man's simple request for a glass of wine to revive him. The king, it is said, blamed his retainers for their discourtesy but upheld his own action. Soon after, the old man died broken-hearted in France. It is said that King Henry

VIII of England chided his nephew James V of Scotland for his sternness, and quoted an old proverb, "A King's face should give grace."

When James, by these somewhat drastic means, had established himself as the real ruler of Scotland, he began to restore order among the various factions of the country. Notorious chieftains were executed, prominent leaders imprisoned, and the disturbing elements crushed. Finally the Scotch people learned that their king insisted upon law and order and gave him their allegiance.

James kept in touch with his kingdom by going in disguise to various sections. Dressed as an ordinary farmer, he toured the country to discover any dissatisfaction or unrest which might exist among the people. When he returned to his castle, he did everything that he thought would add to the peace and security of Scotland. His methods would seem to us, today, to be unnecessarily cruel and relentless, but we must remember the type of men he had to deal with before we judge him too harshly. It was on one of the trips in disguise that we find him following the stag at the beginning of *The Lady of the Lake*.

SIR RODERICK DHU

Sir Roderick was the outlawed chief of the supposed Highland clan, Vich Alpine. The MacGregor clan corresponds to the imaginary Vich Alpine which Scott describes in the poem. Sir Roderick ruled over the territory near the Trossachs, Loch Katrine, and Ben Ledi.

JAMES DOUGLAS

In the poem we recognize James Douglas as Archibald Douglas of Kilspindie, an uncle of the Earl of Angus. All members of the Douglas clan were outlawed, and their lands and chattels confiscated, because of the hatred that existed between the king and the house of Angus.

ELLEN DOUGLAS

Ellen Douglas, the Lady of the Lake in the poem, was the daughter of James Douglas. Ellen and her father, noble exiles, were under the protection of Sir Roderick Dhu.

MALCOLM GRAEME

Malcolm Graeme, a powerful young chieftain, was Ellen's chosen lover. His family held property in Stirlingshire. Sir John Graham, the friend of Wallace, and the famous Marquis of Montrose, Graham of Cloverhouse, as well as many others prominent in the history of Scotland were connected with this family.

BLANCHE OF DEVAN

Blanche of Devan was a captive maid whom Sir Roderick had carried away. Owing chiefly to her capture, she became mentally unbalanced.

RED MURDOCK

Red Murdock was James Fitz-James's treacherous Highland guide.

ALLAN-BANE

Allan-bane, an old harper and minstrel, was a faithful friend and follower of the Douglas family.

LADY MARGARET

Lady Margaret was the mother of the chieftain, Sir Roderick Dhu, and an aunt of Ellen.

BRIAN

Brian was an old monk, connected with Clan Alpine. He was supposed to have supernatural power.

THE LADY OF THE LAKE

CANTO FIRST

THE CHASE

HARP of the North [1] that mouldering long hast hung
  On the witch-elm [2] that shades Saint Fillan's
    spring, [3]
And down the fitful breeze thy numbers [4] flung,
  Till envious ivy did around thee cling,
Muffling with verdant ringlet every string, —   5
  O Minstrel Harp, still must thine accents sleep?
Mid rustling leaves and fountains murmuring,
  Still must thy sweeter sounds their silence keep,
Nor bid a warrior smile, nor teach a maid to weep?

Not thus, in ancient days of Caledon, [5]   10
  Was thy voice mute amid the festal crowd,
When lay [6] of hopeless love, or glory won,
  Aroused the fearful, or subdued the proud.
At each according pause, [7] was heard aloud
  Thine ardent symphony sublime and high!   15
Fair dames and crested chiefs attention bow'd;
  For still the burden of thy minstrelsy [8]
Was Knighthood's dauntless deed, and Beauty's
    matchless eye.

---

[1] The early Scotch minstrels accompanied their songs with the harp.
[2] a drooping elm resembling our weeping willow, whose twigs were used as divining-rods.
[3] Scotch abbot, eighth century, a favorite saint of Robert Bruce. People were often dipped in his spring to cure insanity.   [4] verses
[5] The Romans called Scotland, Caledonia.   [6] song
[7] a pause in the singing   [8] subject of the song

O wake once more! how rude soe'er the hand
    That ventures o'er thy magic maze to stray;   20
O wake once more! though scarce my skill command
    Some feeble echoing of thine earlier lay:
Though harsh and faint, and soon to die away,
    And all unworthy of thy nobler strain,
Yet if one heart throb higher at its sway,   25
    The wizard note has not been touch'd in vain.
Then silent be no more!   Enchantress, [1] wake again!

I

    The stag at eve had drunk his fill,
    Where danced the moon on Monan's rill, [2]
    And deep his midnight lair had made   30
    In lone Glenartney's [3] hazel shade;
    But, when the sun his beacon red
    Had kindled on Ben Voirlich's [4] head,
    The deep-mouth'd bloodhound's heavy bay
    Resounded up the rocky way,   35
    And faint, from farther distance borne,
    Were heard the clanging hoof and horn.

II

    As Chief, who hears his warder [5] call,
    "To arms! the foemen storm the wall,"
    The antler'd monarch of the waste   40
    Sprung from his heathery [6] couch in haste.
    But, ere his fleet career he took,
    The dew-drops from his flanks he shook;
    Like crested leader proud and high,
    Toss'd his beam'd frontlet [7] to the sky;   45

[1] poetry   [2] St. Monan was a fourth-century Scotch martyr.
[3] See the map.   [4] *Ben* is Gaelic for "mountain."   [5] watchman
[6] Heather is a small evergreen shrub of the Scottish Highlands.
[7] the stag's forehead.   The stag's head is "beamed" when his fourth-year horns
appear.

A moment gazed adown the dale,
A moment snuff'd the tainted gale,[1]
A moment listen'd to the cry,
That thicken'd as the chase drew nigh;
Then, as the headmost foes appear'd,   50
With one brave bound the copse [2] he clear'd,
And, stretching forward free and far,
Sought the wild heaths of Uam-Var. [3]

III

Yell'd on the view the opening pack; [4]
Rock, glen, and cavern, paid them back;   55
To many a mingled sound at once
The awaken'd mountain gave response.
A hundred dogs bay'd deep and strong,
Clatter'd a hundred steeds along,
Their peal the merry horns rung out,   60
A hundred voices join'd the shout;
With hark and whoop and wild halloo,
No rest Ben Voirlich's echoes knew.
Far from the tumult fled the roe, [5]
Close in her covert cower'd the doe, [6]   65
The falcon, from her cairn [7] on high,
Cast on the rout a wondering eye,
Till far beyond her piercing ken
The hurricane had swept the glen.
Faint, and more faint, its failing din   70
Return'd from cavern, cliff, and linn, [8]

---

[1] wind scented with the odor of the hunters
[2] brushwood
[3] a mountain northeast of Callander. The word signifies *big den* or *cavern*.
[4] The hounds barked at the sight of the stag.
[5] small deer
[6] female deer
[7] usually a mound or heap of stones. Scott here means a rocky ledge which the falcon uses in watching for prey.
[8] precipice

And silence settled, wide and still,
On the lone wood and mighty hill.

IV

Less loud the sounds of silvan war
Disturb'd the heights of Uam-Var,   75
And roused the cavern, where, 'tis told,
A giant made his den of old;
For ere that steep ascent was won,
High in his pathway hung the sun,
And many a gallant, stay'd perforce,   80
Was fain to breathe his faltering horse,
And of the trackers of the deer,
Scarce half the lessening pack was near;
So shrewdly [1] on the mountain side,
Had the bold burst their mettle tried.   85

V

The noble stag was pausing now
Upon the mountain's southern brow,
Where broad extended, far beneath,
The varied realms of fair Menteith. [2]
With anxious eye he wander'd o'er   90
Mountain and meadow, moss and moor,
And ponder'd refuge from his toil,
By far Lochard or Aberfoyle. [3]
But nearer was the copsewood grey,
That waved and wept on Loch-Achray, [4]   95
And mingled with the pine-trees blue
On the bold cliffs of Ben Venue. [5]
Fresh vigour with the hope return'd,
With flying foot the heath he spurn'd,
Held westward with unwearied race,   100
And left behind the panting chase.

[1] severely   [2] See map.   [3] See map.   [4] See map.   [5] See map.

VI

'Twere long to tell what steeds gave o'er,
As swept the hunt through Cambusmore: [1]
What reins were tighten'd in despair,
When rose Ben Ledi's ridge in air;   105
Who flagg'd upon Bochastle's heath,
Who shunn'd to stem the flooded Teith, —
For twice that day, from shore to shore,
The gallant stag swam stoutly o'er.
Few were the stragglers, following far,   110
That reach'd the lake of Vennachar,
And when the Brigg of Turk [2] was won,
The headmost horseman rode alone.

VII

Alone, but with unbated zeal,
That horseman plied the scourge and steel; [3]   115
For jaded now, and spent with toil,
Emboss'd [4] with foam, and dark with soil,
While every gasp with sobs he drew,
The labouring stag strain'd full in view.
Two dogs of black Saint Hubert's breed, [5]   120
Unmatch'd for courage, breath, and speed,
Fast on his flying traces came,
And all but won that desperate game;
For, scarce a spear's length from his haunch,
Vindictive toil'd the bloodhounds stanch;   125
Nor nearer might the dogs attain,
Nor farther might the quarry [6] strain.
Thus up the margin of the lake,

[1] an estate about two miles from Callander on the Teith River
[2] the bridge spanning the River Turk
[3] whip and spur   [4] an old hunting term
[5] According to tradition, St. Hubert was a great hunter. After his death the
abbots of his monastery perpetuated his breed of hounds.
[6] the hunted animal

Between the precipice and brake,[1]
O'er stock [2] and rock their race they take.   130

VIII

The Hunter mark'd that mountain [3] high,
The lone lake's western boundary,
And deem'd the stag must turn to bay.[4]
Where that huge rampart barr'd the way;
Already glorying in the prize,   135
Measured his antlers with his eyes;
For the death-wound and death-halloo,
Muster'd his breath, his whinyard [5] drew; —
But thundering as he came prepared,
With ready arm and weapon bared,   140
The wily quarry shunn'd the shock,
And turn'd him [6] from the opposing rock;
Then, dashing down a darksome glen,
Soon lost to hound and Hunter's [7] ken,
In the deep Trossachs' [8] wildest nook   145
His solitary refuge took.
There, while close couch'd, the thicket shed
Cold dews and wild-flowers on his head,
He heard the baffled dogs in vain
Rave through the hollow pass amain,   150
Chiding the rocks that yell'd [9] again.

IX

Close on the hounds the Hunter came,
To cheer them on the vanish'd game;
But, stumbling in the rugged dell,

---

[1] thicket   [2] stumps of trees
[3] Ben Venue   [4] to meet the hunter when escape is impossible
[5] a short thick sword or knife   [6] turned himself
[7] The reason for the capitalization will appear later. Watch for it.
[8] Literally *Trossachs* means "bristling country." See map.
[9] echoed

THE BRIGG OF TURK

From this point on, the Stranger Hunter pursued the stag alone. Photo by Ewing Galloway.

The gallant horse exhausted fell.   155
The impatient rider strove in vain
To rouse him with the spur and rein,
For the good steed, his labours o'er,
Stretch'd his stiff limbs, to rise no more;
Then, touch'd with pity and remorse,   160
He sorrow'd o'er the expiring horse.
"I little thought, when first thy rein
I slack'd upon the banks of Seine,[1]
That Highland eagle e'er should feed
On thy fleet limbs, my matchless steed!   165
Woe worth [2] the chase, woe worth the day,
That costs thy life, my gallant grey!"

X

Then through the dell his horn resounds,
From vain pursuit to call the hounds.
Back limp'd, with slow and crippled pace,   170
The sulky leaders of the chase;
Close to their master's side they press'd,
With drooping tail and humbled crest;
But still the dingle's [3] hollow throat
Prolong'd the swelling bugle-note.   175
The owlets started from their dream,
The eagles answered with their scream,
Round and around the sounds were cast,
Till echo seem'd an answering blast;
And on the Hunter hied [4] his way,   180
To join some comrades of the day;
Yet often paused, so strange the road,
So wondrous were the scenes it show'd.

---

1 the river flowing through Paris
2 from the old verb *weorthan*, "to become." The best meaning here is "alas!"
3 a valley or glen
4 hastened

XI

The western waves of ebbing day
Roll'd o'er the glen their level way; [1]   185
Each purple peak, each flinty spire,
Was bathed in floods of living fire.
But not a setting beam could glow
Within the dark ravines below,
Where twined the path in shadow hid,   190
Round many a rocky pyramid,
Shooting abruptly from the dell
Its thunder-splinter'd pinnacle;
Round many an insulated [2] mass,
The native bulwarks of the pass,   195
Huge as the tower which builders vain
Presumptuous piled on Shinar's plain. [3]
The rocky summits, split and rent,
Form'd turret, dome, or battlement,
Or seem'd fantastically set   200
With cupola or minaret,
Wild crests as pagod [4] ever deck'd,
Or mosque of Eastern architect.
Nor were these earth-born castles bare,
Nor lack'd they many a banner fair;   205
For, from their shiver'd brows display'd,
Far o'er the unfathomable glade, [5]
All twinkling with the dewdrop sheen, [6]
The brier-rose fell in streamers green,
And creeping shrubs, of thousand dyes,   210
Waved in the west-wind's summer sighs.

XII

Boon [7] Nature scatter'd, free and wild,
Each plant or flower, the mountain's child.

[1] the horizontal rays of the setting sun   [2] isolated   [3] Read Genesis xi, 1–9.
[4] pagoda   [5] large open spaces   [6] bright, shining   [7] kind

Here eglantine embalm'd the air,
Hawthorn and hazel mingled there;   215
The primrose pale and violet flower,
Found in each cliff a narrow bower;
Fox-glove and night-shade, side by side,
Emblems of punishment and pride,
Group'd their dark hues with every stain   220
The weather-beaten crags retain.
With boughs that quaked at every breath,
Grey birch and aspen [1] wept beneath;
Aloft, the ash and warrior oak
Cast anchor in the rifted rock;   225
And, higher yet, the pine-tree hung
His shatter'd trunk, and frequent [2] flung,
Where seem'd the cliffs to meet on high,
His bows athwart the narrow'd sky.
Highest of all, where white peaks glanced,   230
Where glist'ning streamers waved and danced,
The wanderer's eye could barely view
The summer heaven's delicious blue;
So wondrous wild, the whole might seem
The scenery of a fairy dream.   235

XIII

Onward, amid the copse 'gan peep
A narrow inlet, still and deep,
Affording scarce such breadth of brim
As served the wild duck's brood to swim.
Lost for a space, through thickets veering,   240
But broader when again appearing,
Tall rocks and tufted knolls their face
Could on the dark-blue mirror trace;
And farther as the Hunter stray'd,

[1] sometimes called the "shivering" or "trembling" poplar
[2] at short intervals

Still broader sweep its channels made.   245
The shaggy mounds no longer stood,
Emerging from entangled wood,
But, wave-encircled, seem'd to float,
Like castle girdled with its moat;
Yet broader floods extending still   250
Divide them from their parent hill,
Till each, retiring, claims to be
An islet in an inland sea.

XIV

And now, to issue from the glen,
No pathway meets the wanderer's ken,   255
Unless he climb, with footing nice,[1]
A far projecting precipice.
The broom's [2] tough roots his ladder made,
The hazel saplings lent their aid;
And thus an airy point he won,   260
Where, gleaming with the setting sun,
One burnish'd sheet of living gold,
Loch Katrine lay beneath him roll'd,
In all her length far winding lay,
With promontory, creek, and bay,   265
And islands that, empurpled bright,
Floated amid the livelier light,
And mountains, that like giants stand,
To sentinel enchanted land.
High on the south, huge Ben Venue   270
Down on the lake in masses threw
Crags, knolls, and mounds, confusedly hurl'd,
The fragments of an earlier world;
A wildering [3] forest feather'd o'er
His ruin'd sides and summit hoar,   275

---

[1] with well-chosen footholds   [2] a shrub   [3] bewildering

While on the north, through middle air,
Ben-Aan [1] heaved high his forehead bare.

XV

From the steep promontory gazed
The stranger, raptured and amazed,
And, "What a scene were here," he cried,   280
"For princely pomp, or churchman's pride!
On this bold brow, a lordly tower;
In that soft vale, a lady's bower;
On yonder meadow, far away,
The turrets of a cloister [2] grey;   285
How blithely might the bugle-horn
Chide, on the lake, the lingering morn!
How sweet, at eve, the lover's lute
Chime, when the groves were still and mute!
And, when the midnight moon should lave   290
Her forehead in the silver wave,
How solemn on the ear would come
The holy matin's distant hum, [3]
While the deep peal's commanding tone
Should wake, in yonder islet lone,   295
A sainted hermit from his cell,
To drop a bead [4] with every knell —
And bugle, lute, and bell, and all,
Should each bewilder'd stranger call
To friendly feast, and lighted hall.   300

XVI

"Blithe were it then to wander here!
But now, — beshrew [5] yon nimble deer, —

---

[1] See map.   [2] monastery
[3] The matin bell first rang at midnight, then later it was changed to daybreak.
It is a summons to morning prayers.
[4] to say a prayer. The word *bead* formerly meant "prayer."
[5] curse

LOCH KATRINE AND ELLEN'S ISLE

Photo by Ewing Galloway.

Like that same hermit's, thin and spare,
The copse must give my evening fare;
Some mossy bank my couch must be,   305
Some rustling oak my canopy.
Yet pass we that; the war and chase
Give little choice of resting-place; —
A summer night, in greenwood spent,
Were but to-morrow's merriment: 310
But hosts may in these wilds abound,
Such as are better miss'd than found;
To meet with Highland plunderers [1] here,
Were worse than loss of steed or deer. —
I am alone; — my bugle-strain   315
May call some straggler of the train;
Or, fall [2] the worst that may betide,
Ere now this falchion [3] has been tried."

XVII

But scarce again his horn he wound,[4]
When lo! forth starting at the sound,   320
From underneath an aged oak,
That slanted from the islet rock,
A damsel guider of its way,
A little skiff shot to the bay,
That round the promontory steep   325
Led its deep line in graceful sweep,
Eddying, in almost viewless wave,
The weeping willow-twig to lave,
And kiss, with whispering sound and slow,
The beach of pebbles bright as snow.   330
The boat had touch'd this silver strand,
Just as the Hunter left his stand,

[1] The clans of this region often swooped down on their Lowland neighbors to steal cattle, burn houses, and even to carry off captives for ransom.
[2] or if the worst happens
[3] knife, sword   [4] blew

And stood conceal'd amid the brake,
To view this Lady of the Lake.
The maiden paused, as if again   335
She thought to catch the distant strain.
With head up-raised, and look intent,
And eye and ear attentive bent,
And locks flung back, and lips apart,
Like monument of Grecian art,   340
In listening mood, she seem'd to stand,
The guardian Naiad [1] of the strand.

XVIII

And ne'er did Grecian chisel trace
A Nymph, a Naiad, or a Grace,[2]
Of finer form, or lovelier face!   345
What though the sun, with ardent frown,
Had slightly tinged her cheek with brown, —
The sportive toil, which, short and light,
Had dyed her glowing hue so bright,
Served too in hastier swell to show   350
Short glimpses of a breast of snow:
What though no rule of courtly grace
To measured mood had train'd her pace, —
A foot more light, a step more true,
Ne'er from the heath-flower dash'd the dew;   355
E'en the slight harebell raised its head,
Elastic from her airy tread:
What though upon her speech there hung
The accents of the mountain tongue, —
Those silver sounds, so soft, so dear,[3]   360
The listener held his breath to hear!

---

[1] water nymph
[2] In classic mythology the Graces were three beautiful sisters, attendants of
Venus and Apollo.
[3] Scott probably meant *clear*. His *d*'s and *cl*'s might have been misinterpreted
by the compositor.

XIX

A chieftain's daughter seem'd the maid;
Her satin snood,[1] her silken plaid,[2]
Her golden brooch,[3] such birth betray'd.
And seldom was a snood amid   365
Such wild luxuriant ringlets hid,
Whose glossy black to shame might bring
The plumage of the raven's wing;
And seldom o'er a breast so fair,
Mantled a plaid with modest care,   370
And never brooch the folds combined
Above a heart more good and kind.
Her kindness and her worth to spy,
You need but gaze on Ellen's [4] eye;
Not Katrine, in her mirror blue,   375
Gives back the shaggy banks more true,
Than every free-born glance confess'd
The guileless movements of her breast;
Whether joy danced in her dark eye,
Or woe or pity claim'd a sigh,   380
Or filial love was glowing there,
Or meek devotion pour'd a prayer,
Or tale of injury call'd forth
The indignant spirit of the North.
One only passion unreveal'd,   385
With maiden pride the maid conceal'd,
Yet not less purely felt the flame; —
O! need I tell that passion's name!

XX

Impatient of the silent horn,
Now on the gale her voice was borne: —   390

---

[1] band or ribbon that Scotch maidens wore. After marriage a cap replaced it.
[2] outer garment, usually checkered, of bright woolen cloth that extended to the knees   [3] Only the daughters of nobility could afford to wear a golden brooch.
[4] The Lady of the Lake

"Father!" she cried; the rocks around
Loved to prolong the gentle sound.
A while she paused, no answer came, —
"Malcolm, was thine the blast?" the name
Less resolutely utter'd fell,   395
The echoes could not catch the swell.
"A stranger I," the Huntsman said,
Advancing from the hazel shade.
The maid, alarm'd, with hasty oar,
Push'd her light shallop [1] from the shore,   400
And when a space was gain'd between,
Closer she drew her bosom's screen;
(So forth the startled swan would swing,
So turn to prune [2] his ruffled wing).
Then safe, though flutter'd and amazed,   405
She paused, and on the stranger gazed.
Not his the form, nor his the eye,
That youthful maidens wont to fly. [3]

XXI

On his bold visage middle age
Had slightly press'd its signet [4] sage, [5]   410
Yet had not quench'd the open truth
And fiery vehemence of youth;
Forward and frolic glee was there,
The will to do, the soul to dare,
The sparkling glance, soon blown to fire,   415
Of hasty love, or headlong ire.
His limbs were cast in manly mould,
For hardy sports or contest bold;
And though in peaceful garb array'd,
And weaponless, except his blade,   420
His stately mien as well implied
A high-born heart, a martial pride,

[1] rowboat   [2] arrange   [3] to flee from   [4] stamp   [5] of wisdom

As if a Baron's crest [1] he wore,
And sheathed in armour trode the shore.
Slighting the petty need [2] he show'd,   425
He told of his benighted road; [3]
His ready speech flow'd fair and free,
In phrase of gentlest courtesy;
Yet seem'd that tone, and gesture bland,
Less used to sue than to command.   430

XXII

A while the maid the stranger eyed,
And, reassured, at length replied,
That Highland halls were open still
To wilder'd [4] wanderers of the hill.
"Nor think you unexpected come   435
To yon lone isle, our desert home;
Before the heath had lost the dew,
This morn, a couch [5] was pull'd for you;
On yonder mountain's purple head
Have ptarmigan and heath-cock bled, [6]   440
And our broad nets have swept the mere,
To furnish forth your evening cheer." —
"Now, by the rood, [7] my lovely maid,
Your courtesy has err'd," he said;
"No right have I to claim, misplaced,   445
The welcome of expected guest.
A wanderer, here by fortune tost,
My way, my friends, my courser [8] lost,
I ne'er before, believe me, fair,
Have ever drawn your mountain air,   450
Till on this lake's romantic strand,
I found a fay in fairy land!" —

[1] a feather on the headgear showing rank
[2] need of food   [3] lost road   [4] lost
[5] The Highlanders made their rude couches from heather.
[6] red and black grouse   [7] cross   [8] horse

XXIII

"I well believe," the maid replied,
As her light skiff approach'd the side, —
"I well believe, that ne'er before
Your foot has trod Loch Katrine's shore;   455
But yet, as far as yesternight,
Old Allan-bane [1] foretold your plight, —
A grey-haired sire, whose eye intent
Was on the vision'd future [2] bent.   460
He saw your steed, a dappled [3] grey,
Lie dead beneath the birchen way;
Painted exact your form and mien,
Your hunting suit of Lincoln green, [4]
That tassell'd horn so gaily gilt,   465
That falchion's crooked blade and hilt,
That cap with heron plumage trim,
And yon two hounds so dark and grim.
He bade that all should ready be,
To grace a guest of fair degree; [5]   470
But light I held his prophecy,
And deem'd it was my father's horn,
Whose echoes o'er the lake were borne."

XXIV

The stranger smiled: — "Since to your home
A destined errant [6] knight I come,   475
Announced by prophet sooth [7] and old,
Doom'd, doubtless, for achievement bold,
I'll lightly front [8] each high emprise,[9]
For one kind glance of those bright eyes.
Permit me, first, the task to guide   480
Your fairy frigate o'er the tide."

[1] a soothsayer who prophesied future events   [2] visions of the future
[3] spotted   [4] a kind of cloth made in Lincoln that was worn by hunters
[5] high rank   [6] wandering   [7] true   [8] face   [9] enterprise

The maid, with smile suppress'd and sly,
The toil unwonted [1] saw him try;
For seldom sure, if e'er before,
His noble hand had grasped an oar: 485
Yet with main strength his strokes he drew,
And o'er the lake the shallop flew;
With heads erect, and whimpering cry,
The hounds behind their passage ply.
Nor frequent does the bright oar break   490
The dark'ning mirror of the lake,
Until the rocky isle [2] they reach,
And moor their shallop on the beach.

XXV

The stranger view'd the shore around;
'Twas all so close with copsewood bound,   495
Nor track nor pathway might declare
That human foot frequented there,
Until the mountain-maiden show'd
A clambering unsuspected road,
That winded through the tangled screen,   500
And open'd on a narrow green,
Where weeping birch and willow round
With their long fibres swept the ground.
Here, for retreat in dangerous hour, [3]
Some chief had framed a rustic bower.   505

XXVI

It was a lodge of ample size,
But strange of structure and device;
Of such materials, as around

---

[1] unaccustomed
[2] Ellen's Isle in Loch Katrine
[3] The chieftains had secret caves, huts, or strongholds where they retired after a defeat.

The workman's hand had readiest found.
Lopp'd of their boughs, their hoar trunks bared, 510
And by the hatchet rudely squared,
To give the walls their destined height,
The sturdy oak and ash unite;
While moss and clay and leaves combined
To fence each crevice from the wind.   515
The lighter pine-trees, overhead,
Their slender length for rafters spread,
And wither'd heath and rushes dry
Supplied a russet canopy.
Due westward, fronting to the green,   520
A rural portico was seen,
Aloft on native pillars borne,
Of mountain fir with bark unshorn,
Where Ellen's hand had taught to twine
The ivy and Idæan vine, [1]   525
The clematis, [2] the favour'd flower
Which boasts the name of virgin-bower,
And every hardy plant could bear [3]
Loch Katrine's keen and searching air.
An instant in this porch she stayed,   530
And gaily to the stranger said,
"On heaven and on thy lady call,
And enter the enchanted hall!" [4]

XXVII

"My hope, my heaven, my trust must be,
My gentle guide, in following thee." —   535
He cross'd the threshold — and a clang
Of angry steel that instant rang.
To his bold brow his spirit rush'd,

---

[1] from Mount Ida near Troy, which was noted for its vines
[2] a popular English flower, often called the "virgin-bower"
[3] Notice that a relative pronoun is understood.
[4] She is joking, of course.

But soon for vain alarm he blush'd,
When on the floor he saw display'd,   540
Cause of the din, a naked blade
Dropp'd from the sheath, that careless flung
Upon a stag's huge antlers swung;
For all around, the walls to grace,
Hung trophies of the fight or chase: 545
A target [1] there, a bugle here,
A battle-axe, a hunting spear,
And broadswords, bows, and arrows store,
With the tusk'd trophies of the boar.
Here grins the wolf as when he died,   550
And there the wild-cat's brindled hide
The frontlet of the elk adorns,
Or mantles o'er the bison's horns;
Pennons and flags defaced and stain'd,
That blackening streaks of blood retain'd,   555
And deer-skins, dappled, dun, and white,
With otter's fur and seal's unite,
In rude and uncouth tapestry all,
To garnish forth the silvan hall.

XXVIII

The wondering stranger round him gazed,   560
And next the fallen weapon raised: —
Few were the arms whose sinewy strength,
Sufficed to stretch it forth at length.
And as the brand he poised and sway'd,
"I never knew but one," he said,   565
"Whose stalwart arm might brook [2] to wield
A blade like this in battle-field."
She sigh'd, then smiled and took the word;
"You see the guardian champion's sword:
As light it trembles in his hand,   570

---

[1] a small shield or buckler   [2] be able, endure

As in my grasp a hazel wand;
My sire's tall form might grace the part
Of Ferragus, or Ascabart; [1]
But in the absent giant's hold
Are women now, and menials old."   575

XXIX

The mistress of the mansion came,
Mature of age, a graceful dame;
Whose easy step and stately port
Had well become a princely court,
To whom, though more than kindred knew [2]   580
Young Ellen gave a mother's due.
Meet welcome to her guest she made,
And every courteous rite was paid,
That hospitality could claim,
Though all unask'd his birth and name.   585
Such then the reverence to a guest,
That fellest [3] foe might join the feast,
And from his deadliest foeman's door
Unquestion'd turn, the banquet o'er.
At length his rank the stranger names,   590
"The Knight of Snowdoun, [4] James Fitz-James; [5]
Lord of a barren heritage, [6]
Which his brave sires, from age to age,
By their good swords had held with toil;
His sire had fallen in such turmoil,   595
And he, God wot, [7] was forced to stand
Oft for his right with blade in hand.

[1] two giants of romantic fable
[2] The mother of Roderick Dhu was Dame Margaret, who had been acting as mother to Ellen. Ellen loved her as much as any daughter loves her mother.
[3] most dreadful   [4] an old name for Stirling Castle
[5] In Norman French *fitz* means "son." Though this was not his real name and title, yet, as you will see later, he was entitled to both.
[6] "By the misfortunes of the earlier James' and the internal feuds of the Scottish chiefs, the kingly power had become little more than a name." Scott.
[7] knows

This morning, with Lord Moray's [1] train
He chased a stalwart stag in vain,
Outstripp'd his comrades, miss'd the deer,   600
Lost his good steed, and wander'd here.''

XXX

Fain [2] would the Knight in turn require
The name and state of Ellen's sire.
Well show'd the elder lady's mien,
That courts and cities she had seen;   605
Ellen, though more her looks display'd
The simple grace of silvan maid,
In speech and gesture, form and face,
Show'd she was come of gentle race.
'Twere strange in ruder rank to find   610
Such looks, such manners, and such mind.
Each hint the Knight of Snowdoun gave,
Dame Margaret heard with silence grave;
Or Ellen, innocently gay,
Turn'd all inquiry light away: —   615
"Weird women we! by dale and down [3]
We dwell, afar from tower and town.
We stem the flood, we ride the blast,
On wandering knights our spells we cast;
While viewless minstrels [4] touch the string,   620
'Tis thus our charmed rhymes we sing.''
She sung, and still a harp unseen
Fill'd up the symphony between.

XXXI
Song

"Soldier, rest! thy warfare o'er,
    Sleep the sleep that knows no breaking: 625

---

[1] a half-brother of James V (James Fitz-James)   [2] gladly
[3] hilly land   [4] unseen minstrels

Dream of battled fields no more,
   Days of danger, nights of waking.
In our isle's enchanted hall,
   Hands unseen thy couch are strewing,
Fairy strains of music fall,   630
   Every sense in slumber dewing.[1]
Soldier, rest! thy warfare o'er,
Dream of fighting fields no more:
Sleep the sleep that knows not breaking,
Morn of toil, nor night of waking.   635

"No rude sound shall reach thine ear,
   Armour's clang, or war-steed champing,
Trump nor pibroch [2] summon here
   Mustering clan, or squadron tramping.
Yet the lark's shrill fife may come   640
At the day-break from the fallow, [3]
And the bittern [4] sound his drum,
   Booming from the sedgy shallow.
Ruder sounds shall none be near,
Guards nor warders challenge here,   645
Here's no war-steed's neigh and champing,
Shouting clans or squadrons stamping."

XXXII

She paused — then, blushing, led the lay
To grace the stranger of the day.
Her mellow notes a while prolong   650
The cadence of the flowing song,
Till to her lips in measured frame
The minstrel verse spontaneous came.
"Huntsman, rest! thy chase is done,
   While our slumbrous spells assail ye,   655

[1] refreshing   [2] bagpipe   [3] untilled ground
[4] a small, speckled heron that utters a peculiar booming note in the breeding season

Dream not, with the rising sun,
  Bugles here shall sound reveillé.[1]
Sleep! the deer is in his den;
  Sleep! thy hounds are by thee lying;
Sleep! nor dream in yonder glen,   660
  How thy gallant steed lay dying.
Huntsman, rest! thy chase is done,
Think not of the rising sun,
For at dawning to assail ye,
Here no bugles sound reveillé."   665

XXXIII

The hall was clear'd — the stranger's bed
Was there of mountain heather spread,
Where oft a hundred guests had lain,
And dream'd their forest sports again.
But vainly did the heath-flower shed   670
Its moorland fragrance round his head;
Not Ellen's spell had lull'd to rest
The fever of his troubled breast.
In broken dreams the image rose
Of varied perils, pains, and woes: 675
His steed now flounders in the brake,
Now sinks his barge upon the lake;
Now leader of a broken host,
His standard falls, his honour's lost.
Then, — from my couch may heavenly might   680
Chase that worst phantom of the night! —
Again return'd the scenes of youth,
Of confident undoubting truth;
Again his soul he interchanged
With friends whose hearts were long estranged. 685
They come, in dim procession led,   •

[1] a drum beat or bugle call that notifies soldiers or sailors to rise in the morning

The cold, the faithless, and the dead;
As warm each hand, each brow as gay,
As if they parted yesterday.
And doubt distracts him at the view —   690
O were his senses false or true?
Dream'd he of death, or broken vow,
Or is it all a vision now?

XXXIV

At length, with Ellen in a grove
He seem'd to walk, and speak of love;   695
She listen'd with a blush and sigh,
His suit was warm, his hopes were high,
He sought her yielded hand to clasp,
And a cold gauntlet [1] met his grasp:
The phantom's sex was changed and gone,   700
Upon its head a helmet shone;
Slowly enlarged to giant size,
With darken'd cheek and threatening eyes,
The grisly [2] visage, stern and hoar,
To Ellen still a likeness bore. —   705
He woke, and, panting with affright,
Recall'd the vision of the night.
The hearth's decaying brands were red,
And deep and dusky lustre shed,
Half showing, half concealing, all   710
The uncouth trophies of the hall.
Mid those the stranger fixed his eye,
Where that huge falchion hung on high,
And thoughts on thoughts, a countless throng,
Rush'd, chasing countless thoughts along,   715
Until, the giddy whirl to cure,
He rose, and sought the moonshine pure.

[1] In the Middle Ages warriors used metal gloves that covered the hand and forearm.   [2] weird, horrible

XXXV

The wild-rose, eglantine, and broom,
Wasted around their rich perfume:
The birch-trees wept in fragrant balm,   720
The aspens [1] slept beneath the calm;
The silver light, with quivering glance,
Play'd on the water's still expanse, —
Wild were the heart whose passion's sway
Could rage beneath the sober ray!   725
He felt its calm, that warrior guest,
While thus he communed with his breast: —
" Why is it, at each turn I trace
Some memory of that exiled race?
Can I not mountain-maiden spy,   730
But she must bear the Douglas eye?
Can I not view a Highland brand, [2]
But it must match the Douglas hand?
Can I not frame a fever'd dream,
But still the Douglas is the theme?   735
I'll dream no more — by manly mind
Not even in sleep is will resign'd.
My midnight orisons [3] said o'er,
I'll turn to rest, and dream no more."
His midnight orisons he told,[4]   740
A prayer with every bead of gold,
Consign'd to heaven his cares and woes,
And sunk in undisturb'd repose;
Until the heath-cock shrilly crew,
And morning dawn'd on Ben Venue.   745

[1] Why did Scott especially mention them?
[2] a sword
[3] prayers.   Consult the dictionary for other words from the same root.
[4] repeated, said

CANTO SECOND

THE ISLAND

I

At morn the black-cock trims his jetty wing,[1]
  'Tis morning prompts the linnet's [2] blithest lay,
All Nature's children feel the matin spring
  Of life reviving, with reviving day;
And while yon little bark glides down the bay,   5
  Wafting the stranger on his way again,
Morn's genial influence roused a minstrel grey,
  And sweetly o'er the lake was heard thy strain,
Mix'd with the sounding harp, O white hair'd
    Allan-bane! [3]

II

Song

"Not faster yonder rowers' might
    Flings from their oars the spray,   10
Not faster yonder rippling bright,
That tracks the shallop's course in light,
    Melts in the lake away,
Than men from memory erase
The benefits of former days;   15
Then, stranger, go! good speed the while,
Nor think again of the lonely isle.

"High place to thee in royal court,
    High place in battle line,   20
Good hawk and hound for silvan sport,

---

[1] the black wing of the heath cock
[2] a song bird
[3] It was the custom of chieftains to employ minstrels, bards, or poets. Their principal duty was to recite ancestral accomplishments, to prophesy future events, and to give comfort during times of trouble.

Where beauty sees the brave resort,
    The honour'd meed [1] be thine!
True be thy sword, thy friend sincere,
Thy lady constant, kind, and dear,   25
And lost in love, and friendship's smile
Be memory of the lonely isle.

III

Song (Continued)

"But if beneath yon southern sky
    A plaided stranger roam,
Whose drooping crest and stifled sigh,   30
And sunken cheek and heavy eye,
    Pine for his Highland home;
Then, warrior, then be thine to show
The care that soothes a wanderer's woe;
Remember then thy hap [2] ere while,[3]   35
A stranger in the lonely isle.
"Or if on life's uncertain main
    Mishap [4] shall mar thy sail;
If faithful, wise, and brave in vain,
Woe, want, and exile thou sustain   40
    Beneath the fickle gale;
Waste not a sigh on fortune changed,
On thankless courts, or friends estranged,
But come where kindred worth shall smile,
To greet thee in the lonely isle."   45

IV

As died the sounds upon the tide,
The shallop reach'd the mainland side,
And ere his onward way he took,
The stranger cast a lingering look,

---

[1] reward   [2] fortune   [3] formerly   [4] sea misfortune

Where easily his eye might reach   50
The Harper on the islet beach,
Reclined against a blighted tree,
As wasted, grey, and worn as he.
To minstrel meditation given,
His reverend brow was raised to heaven,   55
As from [1] the rising sun to claim
A sparkle of inspiring flame.
His hand, reclined upon the wire,
Seem'd watching the awakening fire;
So still he sate, as those who wait   60
Till judgment speak the doom of fate;
So still, as if no breeze might dare
To lift one lock of hoary hair;
So still, as life itself were fled,
In the last sound his harp had sped.   65

V

Upon a rock with lichens [2] wild,
Beside him Ellen sate and smiled. —
Smiled she to see the stately drake
Lead forth his fleet upon the lake,
While her vex'd spaniel, from the beach,
Bay'd at the prize beyond his reach?   70
Yet tell me, then, the maid who knows,
Why deepen'd on her cheek the rose? —
Forgive, forgive, Fidelity!
Perchance the maiden smiled to see   75
Yon parting lingerer wave adieu,
And stop and turn to wave anew;
And, lovely ladies, ere your ire
Condemn the heroine of my lyre,
Show me the fair would [3] scorn to spy,   80
And prize such conquest of her eye!

---

[1] as if from   [2] moss   [3] the fair lady who would

VI

While yet he loiter'd on the spot,
It seem'd as Ellen mark'd him not;
But when he turn'd him to the glade,
One courteous parting sign she made;   85
And after, oft the knight would say,
That not when prize of festal [1] day
Was dealt him by the brightest fair,
Who e'er wore jewel in her hair,
So highly did his bosom swell,   90
As at that simple mute farewell.
Now with a trusty mountain-guide,
And his dark stag-hounds by his side,
He parts [2] — the maid, unconscious still,
Watch'd him wind slowly round the hill;   95
But when his stately form was hid,
The guardian in her bosom chid —
"Thy Malcolm! [3] vain and selfish maid!"
'Twas thus upbraiding conscience said, —
"Not so had Malcolm idly hung   100
On the smooth phrase of southern tongue;
Not so had Malcolm strain'd his eye
Another step than thine to spy. —
Wake, Allan-bane," aloud she cried,
To the old Minstrel by her side, —   105
"Arouse thee from thy moody dream!
I'll give thy harp heroic theme,
And warm thee with a noble name;
Pour forth the glory of the Graeme!" [4]
Scarce from her lip the word had rush'd,   110
When deep the conscious maiden blush'd;

[1] This refers to tournaments.
[2] departs
[3] Malcolm was in love with Ellen.
[4] usually *Graham*. This influential family held large tracts of land in Stirling
and Dumbarton Counties.

LOCH KATRINE AND BEN VENUE

The *Rob Roy* carries tourists who come from all English-speaking countries to see the land of the Lady of the Lake.

Photo by Ewing Galloway.

For of his clan, in hall and bower,
Young Malcolm Graeme was held the flower.

VII

The Minstrel waked his harp — three times
Arose the well-known martial chimes,   115
And thrice their high heroic pride
In melancholy murmurs died.
"Vainly thou bid'st, O noble maid,"
Clasping his wither'd hands, he said,
"Vainly thou bid'st me wake the strain,   120
Though all unwont [1] to bid in vain.
Alas! than mine a mightier hand
Has tuned my harp, my strings has spann'd!
I touch the chords of joy, but low
And mournful answer notes of woe;   125
And the proud march, which victors tread,
Sinks in the wailing for the dead.
O well for me, if mine alone
That dirge's deep prophetic tone!
If, as my tuneful fathers said,   130
This harp, which erst [2] Saint Modan sway'd,[3]
Can thus its master's fate foretell,
Then welcome be the minstrel's knell!

VIII

"But ah! dear lady, thus it sigh'd
The eve thy sainted mother died;   135
And such the sounds which, while I strove
To wake a lay of war or love,
Came marring all the festal mirth,
Appalling me who gave them birth,

---

[1] unused   [2] once
[3] Scotch abbot, seventh century. Some believe his harp was handed down to Allan-bane.

And, disobedient to my call,   140
Wail'd loud through Bothwell's [1] banner'd hall,
Ere Douglases, to ruin driven,
Were exiled from their native heaven. —
Oh! if yet worse mishap and woe,
My master's house must undergo,   145
Or aught but weal [2] to Ellen fair,
Brood in these accents of despair,
No future bard, sad Harp! shall fling
Triumph or rapture from thy string;
One short, one final strain shall flow,   150
Fraught [3] with unutterable woe,
Then shiver'd shall thy fragments lie,
Thy master cast him down and die!"

IX

Soothing she answer'd him — "Assuage,
Mine honour'd friend, the fears of age;   155
All melodies to thee are known,
That harp has rung, or pipe [4] has blown,
In Lowland vale or Highland glen,
From Tweed to Spey — what marvel, then,
At times, unbidden notes should rise,   160
Confusedly bound in memory's ties,
Entangling, as they rush along,
The war-march with the funeral song? —
Small ground is now for boding [5] fear;
Obscure, but safe, we rest us here.   165
My sire, in native virtue great,
Resigning lordship, lands, and state,
Not then to fortune more resign'd,
Than yonder oak might give the wind;

---

[1] a ruined castle near the banks of the Clyde nine miles above Glasgow, where the Earls of Angus, the elder branch of the Douglas family, lived
[2] happiness   [3] freighted   [4] bagpipe   [5] predicting

The graceful foliage storms may reave,[1]   170
The noble stem they cannot grieve.
For me," — she stoop'd, and, looking round,
Pluck'd a blue harebell from the ground, —
"For me, whose memory scarce conveys
An image of more splendid days,   175
This little flower, that loves the lea,
May well my simple emblem be;
It drinks heaven's dew as blithe as rose
That in the king's own garden grows;
And when I place it in my hair,   180
Allan, a bard, is bound to swear
He ne'er saw coronet [2] so fair."
Then playfully the chaplet [3] wild
She wreath'd in her dark locks, and smiled.

X

Her smile, her speech, with winning sway,   185
Wiled [4] the old harper's mood away.
With such a look as hermits throw,
When angels stoop to soothe their woe,
He gazed, till fond regret and pride
Thrilled to a tear, then thus replied: 190
"Loveliest and best! thou little know'st
The rank, the honours, thou hast lost!
O might I live to see thee grace,
In Scotland's court, thy birth-right place,[5]
To see my favourite's step advance,   195
The lightest in the courtly dance,
The cause of every gallant's sigh,
And leading star of every eye,

[1] tear away
[2] crown
[3] wreath
[4] beguiled
[5] According to the minstrel Ellen, of noble birth, is an exile with her clan.

And theme of every minstrel's art,
The Lady of the Bleeding Heart!" — [1]   200

XI

"Fair dreams are these," the maiden cried,
(Light was her accent, yet she sigh'd;)
"Yet is this mossy rock to me
Worth splendid chair and canopy;
Nor would my footsteps spring more gay   205
In courtly dance than blithe strathspey,[2]
Nor half so pleased mine ear incline
To royal minstrel's lay as thine.
And then for suitors proud and high,
To bend before my conquering eye, —   210
Thou, flattering bard! thyself wilt say,
That grim Sir Roderick [3] owns its sway.
The Saxon [4] scourge, Clan-Alpine's pride,
The terror of Loch-Lomond's side,
Would, at my suit, thou know'st, delay   215
A Lennox [5] foray — for a day." —

XII

The ancient bard his glee repress'd:
"Ill hast thou chosen theme for jest!
For who, through all this western wild,
Named Black [6] Sir Roderick e'er, and smiled!   220

---

[1] This was the emblem of the Douglas family, to which Ellen belonged. When Robert Bruce died, he bequeathed his heart to James Douglas with the understanding it would be carried on a crusade to the Holy Land. The heart now rests in Melrose Abbey.

[2] Highland dance, deriving its name from the strath or broad valley of the Spey

[3] the leader of the Clan Alpine. He admired Ellen, hated the Knight of Snowdoun, favored the Douglas cause, and disliked the English.

[4] Gael, the name for the Scottish Highlander; Sassenach or Saxon for the Lowlanders

[5] the strip of land owned by the Lennox family near Loch Menteith

[6] Sir Roderick was often called the "Black." In Gaelic Dhu means "black."

In Holy-Rood [1] a knight he slew;
I saw, when back the dirk he drew,
Courtiers give place before the stride
Of the undaunted homicide;
And since, though outlaw'd,[2] hath his hand   225
Full sternly kept his mountain land.
Who else dared give — ah! woe the day,
That I such hated truth should say —
The Douglas, like a stricken deer,
Disown'd by every noble peer,   230
Even the rude refuge we have here?
Alas, this wild marauding Chief [3]
Alone might hazard our relief,
And now thy maiden charms expand,
Looks for his guerdon in thy hand: [4]   235
Full soon may dispensation [5] sought,
To back his suit, from Rome be brought.
Then, though an exile on the hill,
Thy father, as the Douglas, still
Be held in reverence and fear;   240
And though to Roderick thou'rt so dear,
That thou might'st guide with silken thread,
Slave of thy will, this chieftain dread;
Yet, O loved maid, thy mirth refrain!
Thy hand is on a lion's mane." —   245

XIII

"Minstrel," the maid replied, and high
Her father's soul glanced from her eye,
"My debts to Roderick's house I know:

[1] Holyrood Palace at Edinburgh. Roderick was exiled for this wanton act.
[2] An outlaw was an outcast from society. Any one could take his property or
even put him to death without fear of the law.
[3] The exiled Douglas is given shelter by the robber chief.
[4] reward. Hence he expects the hand of Ellen.
[5] Roderick and Ellen were cousins. Hence they could not marry without per-
mission from the Pope.

All that a mother could bestow,
To Lady Margaret's care I owe,   250
Since first an orphan in the wild
She sorrow'd o'er her sister's child; [1]
To her brave chieftain son, from ire
Of Scotland's king who shrouds [2] my sire,
A deeper, holier debt is owed;   255
And, could I pay it with my blood,
Allan! Sir Roderick should command
My blood, my life, — but not my hand.
Rather will Ellen Douglas dwell
A votaress in Maronnan's [3] cell;   260
Rather through realms beyond the sea,
Seeking the world's cold charity,
Where ne'er was spoke a Scottish word,
And ne'er the name of Douglas heard,
An outcast pilgrim will she rove,   265
Than wed the man she cannot love.

XIV

"Thou shakest, good friend, thy tresses grey —
That pleading look, what can it say
But what I own? — I grant him [4] brave,
But wild as Bracklinn's [5] thundering wave;   270
And generous — save vindictive mood,
Or jealous transport, chafe his blood:
I grant him true to friendly band,
As his claymore [6] is to his hand;
But O! that very blade of steel   275
More mercy for a foe would feel

[1] Roderick Dhu was the son of Lady Margaret; Ellen was the daughter of the sister of Lady Margaret.
[2] protects. Obviously Douglas, Ellen's sire, is being protected by Roderick.
[3] a chapel on the eastern side of Loch Lomond
[4] I grant that he is.
[5] See map.
[6] a large sword used by the Gaels

I grant him liberal, to fling
Among his clan the wealth they bring,
When back by lake and glen they wind,
And in the Lowland leave behind,   280
Where once some pleasant hamlet stood,
A mass of ashes slaked [1] with blood,
The hand that for my father fought,
I honour, as his daughter ought;
But can I clasp it reeking red,   285
From peasants slaughter'd in their shed?
No! wildly while his virtues gleam,
They make his passions darker seem,
And flash along his spirit high,
Like lightning o'er the midnight sky.   290
While yet a child, — and children know,
Instinctive taught, the friend and foe, —
I shudder'd at his brow of gloom,
His shadowy plaid, and sable plume;
A maiden grown, I ill could bear   295
His haughty mien and lordly air:
But, if thou join'st a suitor's claim,
In serious mood, to Roderick's name,
I thrill with anguish! or, if e'er
A Douglas knew the word, with fear.   300
To change such odious theme were best, —
What think'st thou of our stranger guest?" —

XV

"What think I of him? — woe the while [2]
That brought such wanderer to our isle!
Thy father's battle-brand, of yore   305
For Tine-man [3] forged by fairy lore,
What time he leagued, no longer foes,

---

[1] quenched   [2] alas the time
[3] Archibald, third Earl of Douglas, *tined* or *lost* all his combats.

His Border spears with Hotspur's bows,
Did, self-unscabbarded, foreshow
The footstep of a secret foe.[1]   310
If courtly spy hath harbour'd here,
What may we for the Douglas fear?
What for this island, deem'd of old
Clan-Alpine's last and surest hold?
If neither spy nor foe, I pray   315
What yet may jealous Roderick say?
— Nay, wave not thy disdainful head,
Bethink thee of the discord dread,
That kindled when at Beltane [2] game
Thou ledst the dance with Malcolm Graeme;   320
Still, though thy sire the peace renew'd,
Smoulders in Roderick's breast the feud;
Beware! — But hark, what sounds are these?
My dull ears catch no faltering breeze,
No weeping birch, nor aspens wake,   325
Nor breath is dimpling in the lake,
Still is the canna's [3] hoary beard,
Yet, by my minstrel faith, I heard —
And hark again! some pipe of war
Sends the bold pibroch from afar."   330

XVI

Far up the lengthen'd lake were spied
Four darkening specks upon the tide,
That, slow enlarging on the view,
Four mann'd and masted barges [4] grew,
And, bearing downwards from Glengyle,[5]   335
Steer'd full upon the lonely isle;

[1] The Knight of Snowdoun is an enemy of Douglas.
[2] a Celtic festival held about the first of May
[3] a grass growing along the shores of the lakes which produces white cottony
bristles   [4] large boats with sails   [5] See map.

The point of Brianchoil [1] they pass'd,
And, to the windward as they cast,
Against the sun they gave to shine
The bold Sir Roderick's banner'd Pine.[2]   340
Nearer and nearer as they bear,
Spears, pikes, and axes flash in air.
Now might you see the tartans brave,[3]
And plaids and plumage dance and wave,
Now see the bonnets [4] sink and rise,   345
As his tough oar the rower plies;
See, flashing at each sturdy stroke,
The wave ascending into smoke;
See the proud pipers on the bow,
And mark the gaudy streamers [5] flow   350
From their loud chanters [6] down, and sweep
The furrow'd bosom of the deep,
As, rushing through the lake amain,
They plied the ancient Highland strain.

XVII

Ever, as on they bore, more loud   355
And louder rung the pibroch proud.
At first sound, by distance tame,
Mellow'd along the waters came,
And, lingering long by cape and bay,
Wail'd every harsher note away,   360
Then bursting bolder on the ear,
The clan's shrill Gathering [7] they could hear;
Those thrilling sounds, that call the might
Of Old Clan-Alpine to the fight.
Thick beat the rapid notes, as when   365

---

[1] a small promontory on the north side of Loch Katrine
[2] an emblem or badge of the clan of Roderick
[3] gay   [4] Scotch caps
[5] ribbons attached to the tubes of the bagpipes
[3] the tubes or pipes of the bagpipes   [7] clan song

The mustering hundreds shake the glen,
And hurrying at the signal dread,
The batter'd earth returns their tread.
Then prelude light, of livelier tone,
Express'd their merry marching on,   370
Ere peal of closing battle rose,
With mingled outcry, shrieks, and blows;
And mimic din of stroke and ward,
As broad sword upon target jarr'd;
And groaning pause, ere yet again,   375
Condensed, the battle yell'd amain;
The rapid charge, the rallying shout,
Retreat borne headlong into rout.
And bursts of triumph, to declare
Clan-Alpine's conquest — all were there.   380
Nor ended thus the strain; but slow
Sunk in a moan prolong'd and low,
And changed the conquering clarion swell,
For wild lament o'er those that fell.

XVIII

The war-pipes ceased; but lake and hill   385
Were busy with their echoes still;
And, when they slept, a vocal strain
Bade their hoarse chorus wake again,
While loud a hundred clansmen raise
Their voices in their Chieftain's praise.   390
Each boatman, bending to his oar,
With measured sweep the burden [1] bore,
In such wild cadence, as the breeze
Makes through December's leafless trees.
The chorus first could Allan know,   395
" Roderick Vich Alpine, ho! iro!"

[1] chorus

And near, and nearer as they row'd,
Distinct the martial ditty flow'd.

XIX

Boat Song

Hail to the Chief who in triumph advances!
  Honour'd and bless'd be the ever-green Pine!   400
Long may the tree, in his banner that glances,
  Flourish, the shelter and grace of our line!
      Heaven send it happy dew,
      Earth lend it sap anew,
Gayly to bourgeon,[1] and broadly to grow,   405
      While every Highland glen
      Sends our shout back agen,[2]
"Roderigh Vich Alpine dhu,[3] ho! ieroe!"

Ours is no sapling, chance-sown by the fountain,
  Blooming at Beltane, in winter to fade;   410
When the whirlwind has stripp'd every leaf on the
    mountain,
  The more shall Clan-Alpine exult in her shade.
      Moor'd in the rifted rock,
      Proof to the tempest's shock,
Firmer he roots him the ruder it blow;   415
      Menteith and Breadalbane, then,
      Echo his praise agen,
"Roderigh Vich Alpine dhu, ho! ieroe!"

XX

Proudly our pibroch has thrill'd in Glen Fruin,
  And Bannochar's groans to our slogan [4] replied;   420
Glen Luss and Ross-dhu, they are smoking in ruin,
  And the best of Loch-Lomond lie dead on her side.

---

[1] bud, sprout   [2] again
[3] "Black Roderick," a descendant of Alpine   [4] battle cry

Widow and Saxon maid
Long shall lament our raid,
Think of Clan-Alpine with fear and with woe;   425
Lennox and Leven-glen [1]
Shake when they hear agen
"Roderigh Vich Alpine dhu, ho! ieroe!"

Row, vassals, row, for the pride of the Highlands!
Stretch to your oars, for the ever-green Pine!   430
O, that the rose-bud [2] that graces yon islands,
Were wreathed in a garland around him to twine!
O that some seedling gem,
Worthy such noble stem,
Honour'd and bless'd in their shadow might grow!   435
Loud should Clan-Alpine then
Ring from her deepmost glen,
"Roderigh Vich Alpine dhu, ho! ieroe!"

XXI

With all her joyful female band,
Had Lady Margaret sought the strand.   440
Loose on the breeze their tresses flew,
And high their snowy arms they threw,
As echoing back with shrill acclaim,
And chorus wild, the Chieftain's name;
While, prompt to please, with mother's art,   445
The darling passion of his heart,
The Dame called Ellen to the strand,
To greet her kinsman ere he land:
"Come, loiterer, come! a Douglas thou,
And shun to wreathe a victor's brow?" —   450
Reluctantly and slow, the maid
The unwelcome summoning obey'd,
And, when a distant bugle rung,

---

[1] in the direction of the Clyde   [2] Ellen

In the mid-path aside she sprung: —
"List, Allan-bane!   From mainland cast   455
I hear my father's signal blast.
Be ours," she cried, "the skiff to guide,
And waft him from the mountain side."
Then, like a sunbeam, swift and bright,
She darted to her shallop light,   460
And, eagerly while Roderick scann'd,
For her dear form, his mother's band,
The islet far behind her lay,
And she had landed in the bay.

XXII

Some feelings are to mortals given,   465
With less of earth in them than heaven:
And if there be a human tear
From passion's dross refined and clear,
A tear so limpid and so meek,
It would not stain an angel's cheek,   470
'Tis that which pious fathers shed
Upon a duteous daughter's head!
And as the Douglas to his breast
His darling Ellen closely press'd,
Such holy drops her tresses steep'd,   475
Though 'twas an hero's eye that weep'd.
Nor while on Ellen's faltering tongue
Her filial welcomes crowded hung,
Mark'd she, that fear (affection's proof)
Still held a graceful youth aloof;   480
No! not till Douglas named his name,
Although the youth was Malcolm Graeme.

XXIII

Allan, with wistful look the while,
Mark'd Roderick landing on the isle;

The Firth of Forth Bridge

The Forth widens out into a great estuary some miles below Stirling, and nowadays any tourist "to the Highlands bound" goes by train across this great structure. Photo by Brown Brothers.

His master piteously he eyed,   485
Then gazed upon the Chieftain's pride,
Then dash'd, with hasty hand, away
From his dimm'd eye the gathering spray;
And Douglas, as his hand he laid
On Malcolm's shoulder, kindly said,   490
"Canst thou, young friend, no meaning spy
In my poor follower's glistening eye?
I'll tell thee: — he recalls the day,
When in my praise he led the lay
O'er the arch'd gate of Bothwell proud,   495
While many a minstrel answer'd loud,
When Percy's Norman pennon,[1] won
In bloody field, before me shone,
And twice ten knights, the least a name
As mighty as yon Chief may claim,   500
Gracing my pomp, behind me came.
Yet trust me, Malcolm, not so proud
Was I of all that marshall'd crowd,
Though the waned crescent [2] own'd my might,
And in my train troop'd lord and knight,   505
Though Blantyre [3] hymn'd her holiest lays,
And Bothwell's bards flung back my praise,
As when this old man's silent tear,
And this poor maid's affection dear,
A welcome give more kind and true,   510
Than aught my better fortunes knew.
Forgive, my friend, a father's boast,
O! it out-beggars [4] all I lost!"

[1] a flag taken by Douglas in a raid which led to the famous Battle of Otterburn in 1388.

[2] Referring to the defeat of Sir Walter Scott, an ancestor of the poet, and his friends, in their attempt to restore James V. Their shield bore a crescent as their insignia.

[3] A priory near Bothwell Castle on the Clyde. A priory is a religious house ranking below an abbey.

[4] Makes all appear poor.

XXIV

Delightful praise! — like summer rose,
That brighter in the dew-drop glows,   515
The bashful maiden's cheek appear'd,
For Douglas spoke, and Malcolm heard.
The flush of shame-faced joy to hide,
The hounds, the hawk, her cares divide;
The loved caresses of the maid   520
The dogs with crouch and whimper paid;
And, at her whistle, on her hand
The falcon took her favourite stand,
Closed his dark wing, relax'd his eye,
Nor, though unhooded,[1] sought to fly.   525
And, trust, while in such guise she stood,
Like fabled Goddess [2] of the wood,
That if a father's partial thought
O'erweigh'd her worth, and beauty aught,
Well might the lover's judgment fail   530
To balance with a juster scale;
For with each secret glance he stole,
The fond enthusiast sent his soul.

XXV

Of stature tall, and slender frame,
But firmly knit, was Malcolm Graeme.   535
The belted plaid and tartan hose
Did ne'er more graceful limbs disclose;
His flaxen hair, of sunny hue,
Curl'd closely round his bonnet blue.
Train'd to the chase, his eagle eye   540
The ptarmigan in snow could spy:
Each pass, by mountain, lake, and heath,

[1] During the Middle Ages hawks were trained to pursue game. They were carried with their heads *hooded*, or covered, before the flight for the prey.
[2] like Diana, the huntress

He knew, through Lennox and Menteith;
Vain was the bound of dark-brown doe,
When Malcolm bent his sounding bow,   545
And scarce that doe, though wing'd with fear,
Outstripp'd in speed the mountaineer:
Right up Ben-Lomond could he press,
And not a sob his toil confess.
His form accorded with a mind   550
Lively and ardent, frank and kind;
A blither heart, till Ellen came,
Did never love nor sorrow tame;
It danced as lightsome in his breast,
As play'd the feather on his crest.   555
Yet friends, who nearest knew the youth,
His scorn of wrong, his zeal for truth,
And bards, who saw his features bold,
When kindled by the tales of old,
Said, were that youth to manhood grown,   560
Not long should Roderick Dhu's renown
Be foremost voiced by mountain fame,
But quail to that of Malcolm Graeme.

XXVI

Now back they wend their watery way,
And, "O my sire!" did Ellen say,   565
"Why urge thy chase so far astray?
And why so late return'd?   And why" —
The rest was in her speaking eye.
"My child, the chase I follow far,
'Tis mimicry of noble war;   570
And with that gallant pastime reft
Were all of Douglas I have left.
I met young Malcolm as I stray'd
Far eastward, in Glenfinlas' shade,
Nor stray'd I safe; for, all around,   575

Hunters and horsemen scour'd the ground.
This youth, though still a royal ward,[1]
Risk'd life and land to be my guard,
And through the passes of the wood
Guided my steps, not unpursued;   580
And Roderick shall his welcome make,
Despite old spleen,[2] for Douglas' sake.
Then must he seek Strath-Endrick glen,
Nor peril aught[3] for me agen."

XXVII

Sir Roderick, who to meet them came,   585
Redden'd at sight of Malcolm Graeme,
Yet, not in action, word, or eye,
Fail'd aught in hospitality.
In talk and sport they whiled away
The morning of that summer day;   590
But at high noon a courier light
Held secret parley with the knight,
Whose moody aspect soon declared,
That evil were the news[4] he heard.
Deep thought seem'd toiling in his head;   595
Yet was the evening banquet made,
Ere he assembled round the flame,[5]
His mother, Douglas, and the Graeme,
And Ellen, too; then cast around
His eyes, then fix'd them on the ground,   600
As studying phrase that might avail
Best to convey unpleasant tale.
Long with his dagger's hilt he play'd,
Then raised his haughty brow, and said: —

[1] As yet Malcolm was under age. The king was the guardian of such noble
orphans.
[2] feud   [3] cause any peril
[4] In the days of Scott this word was used either as singular or plural.
[5] hearth, fireplace

XXVIII

"Short be my speech; — nor time affords,   605
Nor my plain temper, glozing [1] words.
Kinsman and father, — if such name
Douglas vouchsafe to Roderick's claim;
Mine honour'd mother: — Ellen — why,
My cousin, turn away thine eye? —   610
And Graeme; in whom I hope to know
Full soon a noble friend or foe,
When age shall give thee thy command,
And leading in thy native land, —
List all! — The King's vindictive pride   615
Boasts to have tamed the Border-side,
Where chiefs, with hound and hawk who came
To share their monarch's silvan game,
Themselves in bloody toils were snared;
And when the banquet they prepared,   620
And wide their loyal portals flung,
O'er their own gateway struggling hung. [2]
Loud cries their blood from Meggat's mead,
From Yarrow braes, and banks of Tweed,
Where the lone streams of Ettrick glide,   625
And from the silver Teviot's side;
The dales, where martial clans did ride,
Are now one sheep-walk, [3] waste and wide.
This tyrant of the Scottish throne,
So faithless, and so ruthless known,   630
Now hither comes; his end the same,
The same *pretext* of silvan game.
What grace [4] for Highland Chiefs, judge ye
By fate of Border chivalry.
Yet more; amid Glenfinlas green,   635
Douglas, thy stately form was seen.

---

[1] flattering   [2] The messenger brought this story.   [3] pasture   [4] pardon

This by *espial* [1] sure I know:
Your counsel in the *streight* [2] I show."

XXIX

Ellen and Margaret fearfully
Sought comfort in each other's eye,   640
Then turn'd their ghastly look, each one,
This to her sire, that to her son.
The hasty colour went and came
In the bold cheek of Malcolm Graeme;
But from his glance it well appear'd,   645
'Twas but for Ellen that he fear'd;
While, sorrowful, but undismay'd,
The Douglas thus his counsel said: —
"Brave Roderick, though the tempest roar,
It may but thunder and pass o'er;   650
Nor will I here remain an hour,
To draw the lightning on thy bower;
For well thou know'st, at this grey head
The royal bolt were fiercest sped.
For thee, who, at thy King's command,   655
Canst aid him with a gallant band,
Submission, homage, humbled pride,
Shall turn the Monarch's wrath aside.
Poor remnants of the Bleeding Heart,
Ellen and I will seek, apart,   660
The refuge of some forest cell,
There, like the hunted *quarry*, dwell,
Till on the mountain and the *moor*,
The stern pursuit be pass'd and o'er." —

XXX

"No, by mine honour," Roderick said,   665
"So help me Heaven, and my good blade!

[1] spying   [2] strait; difficulty

No, never! Blasted be yon Pine,
My fathers' ancient crest and mine,
If from its shade in danger part
The *lineage* of the Bleeding Heart!   670
Hear my blunt speech: Grant me this maid
To wife, thy counsel to mine aid;
To Douglas, leagued with Roderick Dhu,
Will friends and allies flock enow; [1]
Like cause of doubt, distrust, and grief,   675
Will bind to us each Western Chief.
When the loud pipes my bridal tell,
The Links of Forth [2] shall hear the knell,
The guards shall start in Stirling's [3] porch;
And, when I light the nuptial torch,   680
A thousand villages in flames
Shall scare the slumbers of King James!
— Nay, Ellen, blench not thus away,
And, mother, cease these signs, I pray;
I meant not all my heart might say. —   685
Small need of inroad, or of fight,
When the sage Douglas may unite
Each mountain clan in friendly band,
To guard the passes of their land,
Till the foil'd king, from pathless glen,   690
Shall bootless [4] turn him home agen."

XXXI

There are who have,[5] at midnight hour,
In slumber scaled a dizzy tower,
And, on the verge that beetled o'er [6]
The ocean tide's incessant roar,   695
Dream'd calmly out their dangerous dream,

---

[1] enough   [2] the windings of the River Forth near Stirling
[3] the gate of Stirling Castle   [4] unsuccessful
[5] there are *those* who have   [6] overhung

Till waken'd by the morning beam;
When, dazzled by the eastern glow,
Such startler [1] cast his glance below,
And saw unmeasured depth around,   700
And heard unintermitted sound,
And thought the battled fence [2] so frail,
It waved like cobweb in the gale; —
Amid his senses' giddy wheel,
Did he not desperate impulse feel,   705
Headlong to plunge himself below,
And meet the worst his fears foreshow? —
Thus, Ellen, dizzy and astound, [3]
As sudden ruin yawn'd around,
By crossing [4] terrors wildly toss'd,   710
Still for the Douglas fearing most,
Could scarce the desperate thought withstand,
To buy his safety with her hand.

XXXII

Such purpose dread could Malcolm spy
In Ellen's quivering lip and eye,   715
And eager rose to speak — but ere
His tongue could hurry forth his fear,
Had Douglas mark'd the hectic strife,
Where death seem'd combating with life;
For to her cheek, in feverish flood,   720
One instant rush'd the throbbing blood,
Then ebbing back, with sudden sway,
Left its domain as wan as clay.
"Roderick, enough! enough!" he cried,
"My daughter cannot be thy bride;   725
Not that the blush to wooer dear,
Nor paleness that of maiden fear.
It may not be — forgive her, Chief,

---

[1] startled dreamer [2] battlemented rampart [3] astounded [4] conflicting

Nor hazard aught for our relief.
Against his sovereign, Douglas ne'er   730
Will level a rebellious spear.
'Twas I that taught his youthful hand
To rein a steed and wield a brand;
I see him yet, the princely boy!
Not Ellen more my pride and joy;   735
I love him still, despite my wrongs,
By hasty wrath, and slanderous tongues.
O seek the grace you well may find,
Without a cause to mine combined."

XXXIII

Twice through the hall the Chieftain strode;   740
The waving of his tartans broad,
And darken'd brow, where wounded pride
With ire and disappointment vied,
Seem'd, by the torch's gloomy light,
Like the ill Demon of the night,   745
Stooping his pinions' shadowy sway
Upon the nighted [1] pilgrim's way:
But, unrequited Love! thy dart
Plunged deepest its envenom'd smart,
And Roderick, with thine anguish stung,   750
At length the hand of Douglas wrung,
While eyes, that mock'd at tears before,
With bitter drops were running o'er.
The death-pangs of long-cherish'd hope
Scarce in that ample breast had scope,   755
But, struggling with his spirit proud,
Convulsive heaved its chequer'd shroud,[2]
While every sob — so mute were all —
Was heard distinctly through the hall.
The son's despair, the mother's look,   760

[1] benighted   [2] his Tartan plaid or garment

Ill might the gentle Ellen brook; [1]
She rose, and to her side there came,
To aid her parting [2] steps, the Graeme.

XXXIV

Then Roderick from the Douglas broke —
As flashes flame through sable smoke,   765
Kindling its wreaths, long, dark, and low,
To one broad blaze of ruddy glow,
So the deep anguish of despair
Burst, in fierce jealousy, to air.
With stalwart grasp his hand he laid   770
On Malcolm's breast and belted plaid:
"Back, beardless boy!" he sternly said,
"Back, minion! [3] hold'st thou thus at naught
The lesson I so lately taught?
This roof, the Douglas, and that maid,   775
Thank thou for punishment delay'd."
Eager as greyhound on his game
Fiercely with Roderick grappled Graeme.
"Perish my name, if aught afford
Its Chieftain's safety save his sword!"   780
Thus as they strove, their desperate hand
Griped to the dagger or the brand,
And death had been — but Douglas rose,
And thrust between the struggling foes
His giant strength: — "Chieftains, forego!   785
I hold the first who strikes, my foe. —
Madmen, forbear your frantic jar! [4]
What! is the Douglas fall'n so far,
His daughter's hand is doom'd the spoil
Of such dishonourable broil!"   790
Sullen and slowly they unclasp,

---

[1] endure   [2] departing   [3] servant, slave   [4] desperate struggle

Dryburgh Abbey

Once owned by Sir Walter Scott's family, where Scott and his family lie buried.
No matter how poor the Scots were in early days, they erected beautiful churches,
as the ruins show.   Photo by Brown Brothers.

As struck with shame, their desperate grasp,
And each upon his rival glared,
With foot advanced, and blade half bared.

XXXV

Ere yet the brands aloft were flung   795
Margaret on Roderick's mantle hung,
And Malcolm heard his Ellen's scream,
As falter'd through terrific dream.
Then Roderick plunged in sheath his sword
And veil'd his wrath in scornful word: 800
"Rest safe till morning; pity t'were
Such cheek should feel the midnight air!
Then mayest thou to James Stuart tell,
Roderick will keep the lake and fell,[1]
Nor lackey,[2] with his freeborn clan,   805
The pageant pomp of earthly man.
More would he of Clan-Alpine know,
Thou canst our strength and passes show. —
Malise, what ho!" — his henchman[3] came;
"Give our safe-conduct[4] to the Graeme."   810
Young Malcolm answer'd, calm and bold,
"Fear nothing for thy favourite hold;
The spot, an angel deigned to grace,
Is bless'd, though robbers haunt the place.
Thy churlish courtesy for those   815
Reserve, who fear to be thy foes.
As safe to me the mountain way
At midnight as in blaze of day,
Though with his boldest at his back
Even Roderick Dhu beset the track. —   820
Brave Douglas, — lovely Ellen, — nay,
Nought here of parting will I say.

[1] mountain region   [2] be a slave to
[3] a chieftain's attendant   [4] passport

Earth does not hold a lonesome glen,
So secret, but we meet agen. —
Chieftain! we too shall find an hour," [1]   825
He said, and left the silvan bower.

XXXVI

Old Allan follow'd to the strand,
(Such was the Douglas's command,)
And anxious told, how, on the morn,[2]
The stern Sir Roderick deep had sworn,   830
The Fiery Cross [3] should circle o'er
Dale, glen, and valley, down, and moor.
Much were the peril to the Graeme,
From those who to the signal came;
Far up the lake 'twere safest land,   835
Himself would row him to the strand.
He gave his counsel to the wind,
While Malcolm did, unheeding, bind,
Round dirk and pouch and broadsword roll'd,
His ample plaid in tighten'd fold,   840
And stripp'd his limbs to such array,
As best might suit the watery way, —

XXXVII

Then spoke abrupt: "Farewell to thee,
Pattern of old fidelity!"
The Minstrel's hand he kindly press'd, —   845
"O! could I point [4] a place of rest!
My sovereign holds in ward my land,
My uncle leads my vassal band;
To tame his foes, his friends to aid,
Poor Malcolm has but heart and blade.   850

---

[1] find the time and place for combat
[2] on the morn. This modifies *should circle* and not the nearer verb *had sworn.*
[3] the signal that calls the clan for battle   [4] point out

Yet, if there be one faithful Graeme,
Who loves the chieftain of his name,
Not long shall honour'd Douglas dwell,
Like hunted stag in mountain cell;
Nor, ere yon pride-swoll'n robber dare, — 855
I may not give the rest to air!
Tell Roderick Dhu, I owed him nought,
Not the poor service of a boat,
To waft me to yon mountain-side."
Then plunged he in the flashing tide. 860
Bold o'er the flood his head he bore,
And stoutly steer'd him from the shore;
And Allan strain'd his anxious eye,
Far 'mid the lake his form to spy.
Darkening across each puny wave, 865
To which the moon her silver gave,
Fast as the cormorant could skim,
The swimmer plied each active limb;
Then landing in the moonlight dell,
Loud shouted of his weal to tell. 870
The Minstrel heard the far halloo,
And joyful from the shore withdrew.[1]

CANTO THIRD

THE GATHERING

I

TIME rolls his ceaseless course. The race of yore,
    Who danced our infancy upon their knee,
And told our marvelling boyhood legends store,
    Of their strange ventures happ'd by land or sea,
How are they blotted from the things that be! 5

[1] Did you observe that this canto closed with evening and moonlight? You will recall that Canto I ended with morning.

How few, all weak and wither'd of their force,
Wait on the verge of dark eternity,
  Like stranded wrecks, the tide returning hoarse,
To sweep them from our sight! Time rolls his cease-
      less course.

Yet live there still who ¹ can remember well,   10
  How, when a mountain chief his bugle blew,
Both field and forest, dingle,² cliff, and dell,
  And solitary heath, the signal knew;
And fast the faithful clan around him drew,
  What time ³ the warning note was keenly wound,⁴   15
What time aloft their kindred banner flew,
  While clamorous war-pipes yell'd the gathering
      sound,⁵
And while the Fiery Cross glanced, like a meteor,
      round.

II

  The Summer dawn's reflected hue
  To purple changed Loch Katrine blue;   20
  Mildly and soft the western breeze
  Just kiss'd the lake, just stirr'd the trees,
  And the pleased lake, like maiden coy,
  Trembled but dimpled not for joy;
  The mountain-shadows on her breast   25
  Were neither broken nor at rest;
  In bright uncertainty they lie,
  Like future joys to Fancy's eye.⁶
  The water-lily to the light
  Her chalice rear'd of silver bright;   30
  The doe awoke, and to the lawn,
  Begemm'd with dew-drops, led her fawn;
  The grey mist left the mountain-side,

¹ still those who   ² a secluded valley   ³ when
⁴ sounded   ⁵ summoning the clan   ⁶ imagination

The torrent show'd its glistening pride;
Invisible in flecked sky,   35
The lark sent down her revelry; [1]
The blackbird and the speckled thrush
Good-morrow gave from brake and bush;
In answer coo'd the cushat dove
Her notes of peace, and rest, and love.   40

III

No thought of peace, no thought of rest,
Assuaged the storm in Roderick's breast.
With sheathed broadsword in his hand,
Abrupt he paced the islet strand,
And eyed the rising sun, and laid   45
His hand on his impatient blade.
Beneath a rock, his vassals' care
Was prompt the ritual [2] to prepare,
With deep and deathful meaning fraught;
For such Antiquity had taught   50
Was preface meet, ere yet abroad
The Cross of Fire should take its road.
The shrinking band stood oft aghast
At the impatient glance he cast; —
Such glance the mountain eagle threw,   55
As, from the cliffs of Ben Venue,
She spread her dark sails on the wind,
And, high in middle heaven reclined,
With her broad shadow on the lake,
Silenced the warblers of the brake.   60

IV

A heap of wither'd boughs was piled,
Of juniper and rowan [3] wild,

---

[1] morning song of the skylark   [2] religious ceremony   [3] mountain ash

Mingled with shivers [1] from the oak,
Rent by the lightning's recent stroke.
Brian, the Hermit, by it stood,   65
Barefooted, in his frock and hood.
His grisled beard and matted hair
Obscured a visage of despair;
His naked arms and legs, seam'd o'er,
The scars of frantic penance bore.   70
That monk, of savage form and face,
The impending danger of his race
Had drawn from deepest solitude,
Far in Benharrow's bosom rude.
Not his the mien of Christian priest,   75
But Druid's,[2] from the grave released,
Whose harden'd heart and eye might brook
On human sacrifice to look;
And much, 'twas said, of heathen lore
Mix'd in the charms he mutter'd o'er.   80
The hallow'd creed gave only worse
And deadlier emphasis of curse;
No peasant sought that Hermit's prayer,
His cave the pilgrim shunn'd with care,
The eager huntsman knew his bound,   85
And in mid chase call'd off his hound;
Or if, in lonely glen or strath,[3]
The desert-dweller met his path,
He pray'd, and sign'd the cross between,[4]
While terror took devotion's mien.   90

V

Of Brian's birth strange tales were told.
His mother watch'd a midnight fold,[5]
Built deep within a dreary glen,

---

[1] splinters   [2] Celtic Priests   [3] a valley
[4] made the sign of the cross   [5] sheep pen

Where scatter'd lay the bones of men,
In some forgotten battle slain,   95
And bleach'd by drifting wind and rain.
It might have tamed a warrior's heart,
To view such mockery of his art!
The knot-grass fetter'd there the hand,
Which once could burst an iron band;   100
Beneath the broad and ample bone,
That buckler'd heart to fear unknown,
A feeble and a timorous guest,
The field-fare [1] framed her lowly nest;
There the slow blind-worm left his slime   105
On the fleet limbs that mock'd at time;
And there, too, lay the leader's skull,
Still wreathed with chaplet, flush'd and full,
For heath-bell with her purple bloom,
Supplied the bonnet and the plume.   110
All night, in this sad glen, the maid
Sate, shrouded in her mantle's shade:
She said, no shepherd sought her side,
No hunter's hand her snood untied,
Yet ne'er again to braid her hair   115
The virgin snood [2] did Alice wear;
Gone was her maiden glee and sport,
Her maiden girdle all too short,
Nor sought she, from that fatal night,
Or holy church or blessed rite,   120
But lock'd her secret in her breast,
And died in travail, unconfess'd.

VI

Alone, among his young compeers,
Was Brian from his infant years;

[1] a small brownish thrush
[2] a fillet that unmarried women wore about the hair

A moody and heart-broken boy,   125
Estranged from sympathy and joy,
Bearing each taunt which careless tongue
On his mysterious lineage flung.
Whole nights he spent by moonlight pale,
To wood and stream his hap to wail,   130
Till, frantic, he as truth received
What of his birth the crowd believed,
And sought, in mist and meteor fire,
To meet and know his Phantom Sire![1]
In vain, to soothe his wayward fate,   135
The cloister oped her pitying gate;
In vain, the learning of the age
Unclasp'd the sable-letter'd[2] page;
Even in its treasures he could find
Food for the fever of his mind.   140
Eager he read whatever tells
Of magic, cabala,[3] and spells,
And every dark pursuit allied
To curious and presumptuous pride;
Till with fired brain and nerves o'erstrung,   145
And heart with mystic horrors wrung,
Desperate he sought Benharrow's den,
And hid him from the haunts of men.

VII

The desert gave him visions wild,
Such as might suit the spectre's child.
Where with black cliffs the torrents toil,   150
He watch'd the wheeling eddies boil,
Till, from their foam, his dazzled eyes
Beheld the River Demon[4] rise;

[1] mysterious father
[2] Old English letters were much heavier than modern.
[3] mysteries
[4] an evil spirit that foretold misfortune and haunted lakes and streams

LOCH LOMOND

Courtesy of the London and Northeastern Railway.

The mountain mist took form and limb,   155
Of noontide hag,[1] or goblin grim;
The midnight wind came wild and dread,
Swell'd with the voices of the dead;
Far on the future battle-heath
His eyes beheld the ranks of death: 160
Thus the lone Seer, from mankind hurl'd,
Shaped forth a disembodied world.
One lingering sympathy of mind
Still bound him to the mortal kind;
The only parent he could claim   165
Of ancient Alpine lineage came.
Late had he heard, in prophet's dream,
The fatal Ben-Shie's [2] boding scream;
Sounds, too, had come in midnight blast,
Of charging steeds, careering fast   170
Along Benharrow's shingly side,
Where mortal horseman ne'er might ride;
The thunderbolt had split the pine,—
All augur'd ill to Alpine's line.
He girt his loins, and came to show   175
The signals of impending woe,
And now stood prompt to bless or ban,
As bade the Chieftain of his clan.

VIII

'Twas all prepared; — and from the rock,
A goat, the patriarch of the flock,   180
Before the kindling pile was laid,
And pierced by Roderick's ready blade.
Patient the sickening victim eyed
The life-blood ebb in crimson tide,
Down his clogg'd beard and shaggy limb,   185

---

[1] a witch that came at high noon to perform her evil charms
[2] a spirit whose wailing was a sign of death

Till darkness glazed his eyeballs dim.
The grisly priest, with murmuring prayer,
A slender crosslet form'd with care,
A cubit's [1] length in measure due;
The shaft and limbs were rods of yew,   190
Whose parents in Inch-Cailliach [2] wave
Their shadows o'er Clan-Alpine's grave,
And, answering Lomond's breezes deep,
Soothe many a chieftain's endless sleep.
The Cross, thus form'd, he held on high,   195
With wasted hand, and haggard eye,
And strange and mingled feelings woke,
While his anathema he spoke.

IX

"Woe to the clansman, who shall view
This symbol of sepulchral yew, [3]   200
Forgetful that its branches grew
Where weep the heavens their holiest dew
          On Alpine's dwelling low!
Deserter of his Chieftain's trust,
He ne'er shall mingle with their dust,   205
But, from his sires and kindred thrust,
Each clansman's execration just
          Shall doom him wrath and woe."
He paused; — the word the vassals took,
With forward step and fiery look,   210
On high their naked brands they shook,
Their clattering targets wildly strook; [4]
          And first in murmur low,
Then, like the billow in his course,
That far to seaward finds his source,   215

---

[1] eighteen inches
[2] a small island in Loch Lomond where the descendants of King Alpine were buried
[3] a cross made from the yew tree   [4] the old past tense of *strike*

And flings to shore his muster'd force,
Burst, with loud roar, their answer hoarse,
            "Woe to the traitor, woe!"
Ben Aan's grey scalp the accents knew,
The joyous wolf from cover drew,   220
The exulting eagle scream'd afar, —
They knew the voice of Alpine's war.

X

The shout was hush'd on lake and fell,
The Monk resumed his mutter'd spell:
Dismal and low its accents came,   225
The while he scathed [1] the Cross with flame:
And the few words that reach'd the air,
Although the holiest name was there,
Had more of blasphemy than prayer.
But when he shook above the crowd   230
Its kindled points, he spoke aloud: —
"Woe to the wretch, who fails to rear
At this dread sign the ready spear!
For, as the flames this symbol sear,
His home, the refuge of his fear,   235
            A kindred fate shall know;
Far o'er its roof the volumed flame
Clan-Alpine's vengeance shall proclaim,
While maids and matrons on his name
Shall call down wretchedness and shame,   240
            And infamy and woe." [2]
Then rose the cry of females, shrill
As goss-hawk's [3] whistle on the hill,
Denouncing misery and ill,
Mingled with childhood's babbling trill   245
            Of curses stammer'd slow;

[1] scorched
[2] the penalty of the person who failed to support his chieftain
[3] a large hawk with short wings and a sharp shrill call

Answering, with imprecation dread,
"Sunk be his home in embers red!
And cursed be the meanest shed [1]
That e'er shall hide the houseless head,   250
    We doom to want and woe!"
A sharp and shrieking echo gave,
Coir-Uriskin, [2] thy goblin cave!
And the grey pass where birches wave,
    On Beala-nam-bo. [3]   255

XI

Then deeper paused the priest anew,
And hard his labouring breath he drew,
While, with set teeth and clenched hand,
And eyes that glow'd like fiery brand,
He meditated curse more dread,   260
And deadlier, on the clansman's head,
Who, summon'd to his chieftain's aid
The signal saw and disobey'd.
The crosslet's points of sparkling wood,
He quench'd among the bubbling blood.   265
And, as again the sign he rear'd,
Hollow and hoarse his voice was heard:
"When flits this Cross from man to man,
Vich-Alpine's summons to his clan,
Burst be the ear that fails to heed!   270
Palsied the foot that shuns to speed!
May ravens tear the careless eyes,
Wolves make the coward heart their prize!
As sinks that blood-stream in the earth,
So may his heart's blood drench his hearth!   275
As dies in hissing gore the spark,
Quench thou his light, Destruction dark!

[1] home   [2] the name of the Goblin Cave
[3] "the Pass of the Cattle" above the cave

And be the grace [1] to him denied,
Bought by this sign [2] to all beside!"
He ceased; no echo gave agen   280
The murmur of the deep Amen.

XII

Then Roderick, with impatient look,
From Brian's hand the symbol took:
"Speed, Malise, speed!" he said, and gave
The crosslet to his henchman brave.   285
"The muster-place be Lanrick mead —
Instant the time — speed, Malise, speed!"
Like heath-bird, when the hawks pursue,
A barge across Loch Katrine flew;
High stood the henchman on the prow,   290
So rapidly the barge-men row,
The bubbles, where they launched the boat,
Were all unbroken and afloat,
Dancing in foam and ripple still,
When it had near'd the mainland hill;   295
And from the silver beach's side
Still was the prow three fathom wide,
When lightly bounded to the land
The messenger [3] of blood and brand

XIII

Speed, Malise, speed! the dun deer's hide [4]   300
On fleeter foot was never tied.
Speed, Malise, speed! such cause of haste
Thine active sinews never braced.
Bend 'gainst the steepy hill thy breast,

---

[1] forgiveness   [2] sign of the cross
[3] Malise, the henchman of Sir Roderick, who, by showing the Fiery Cross, as-
sembled the clansmen.
[4] The Highlanders wore shoes made of this hide.

Burst down like torrent from its crest;   305
With short and springing footstep pass
The trembling bog and false morass;
Across the brook like roebuck bound,
And thread the brake like questing hound;
The crag is high, the scaur [1] is deep,   310
Yet shrink not from the desperate leap:
Parch'd are thy burning lips and brow
Yet by the fountain pause not now;
Herald of battle, fate, and fear,
Stretch onward in thy fleet career!   315
The wounded hind thou track'st not now,
Pursuest not maid through greenwood bough,
Nor pliest thou now thy flying pace,
With rivals in the mountain race;
But danger, death, and warrior deed,   320
Are in thy course — speed, Malise, speed!

XIV

Fast as the fatal symbol flies,
In arms the huts and hamlets rise;
From winding glen, from upland brown,
They pour'd each hardy tenant down.   325
Nor slack'd the messenger his pace;
He show'd the sign, he named the place,
And, pressing forward like the wind,
Left clamour and surprise behind.
The fisherman forsook the strand,   330
The swarthy smith took dirk and brand; [2]
With changed cheer, [3] the mower blithe
Left in the half-cut swathe the scythe;
The herds without a keeper stray'd,
The plough was in mid-furrow staid,   335

---

[1] cliff   [2] dagger and sword   [3] look

The falc'ner toss'd his hawk away,
The hunter left the stag at bay;
Prompt at the signal of alarms,
Each son of Alpine rush'd to arms;
So swept the tumult and affray   340
Along the margin of Achray.
Alas, thou lovely lake! that e'er
Thy banks should echo sounds of fear!
The rocks, the bosky thickets, sleep
So stilly on thy bosom deep,   345
The lark's blithe carol, from the cloud,
Seems for the scene too gaily loud.

XV

Speed, Malise, speed! the lake is past,
Duncraggan's [1] huts appear at last,
And peep, like moss-grown rocks, half seen,   350
Half hidden in the copse so green;
There mayst thou rest, thy labour done,
Their Lord shall speed the signal on. —
As stoops the hawk upon his prey,
The henchman shot him down the way.   355
— What woeful accents load the gale?
The funeral yell, the female wail!
A gallant hunter's sport is o'er,
A valiant warrior fights no more.
Who, in the battle or the chase,   360
At Roderick's side shall fill his place! —
Within the hall, where torches' ray
Supplies the excluded beams of day,
Lies Duncan [2] on his lowly bier,
And o'er him streams his widow's tear.   365

[1] an estate between Lochs Achray and Vennachar, in the vicinity of the Brigg
of Turk
[2] an active supporter and loyal friend of Sir Roderick

His stripling son stands mournful by,
His youngest weeps, but knows not why;
The village maids and matrons round
The dismal coronach [1] resound.

XVI

Coronach

He is gone on the mountain,   370
  He is lost to the forest,
Like a summer-dried fountain,
  When our need was the sorest.
The font, reappearing,
  From the rain-drops shall borrow,   375
But to us comes no cheering,
  To Duncan no morrow!
The hand of the reaper
  Takes the ears that are hoary,
But the voice of the weeper   380
  Wails manhood in glory.
The autumn winds rushing
  Waft the leaves that are searest,
But our flower was in flushing,[2]
  When blighting was nearest.   385
Fleet foot on the correi,[3]
  Sage counsel in cumber,[4]
Red hand in the foray,
  How sound is thy slumber!
Like the dew on the mountain,   390
  Like the foam on the river,
Like the bubble on the fountain
  Thou art gone, and for ever!

---

[1] a Scottish funeral song
[2] full bloom
[3] "the hollow side of the hill where game usually lies." Scott.
[4] trouble

XVII

See Stumah, who, the bier beside,
His master's corpse with wonder eyed,   395
Poor Stumah! whom his least halloo
Could send like lightning o'er the dew,
Bristles his crest, and points his ears,
As if some stranger step he hears.
'Tis not a mourner's muffled tread,   400
Who comes to sorrow o'er the dead,
But headlong haste, or deadly fear,
Urge the precipitate career.
All stand aghast: — unheeding all,
The henchman bursts into the hall;   405
Before the dead man's bier he stood;
Held forth the Cross besmear'd with blood;
"The muster-place is Lanrick mead;
Speed forth the signal! clansmen, speed!"

XVIII

Angus, the heir of Duncan's line,   410
Sprung forth and seized the fatal sign.
In haste the stripling to his side
His father's dirk and broadsword tied;
But when he saw his mother's eye
Watch him in speechless agony,   415
Back to her open'd arms he flew,
Press'd on her lips a fond adieu —
"Alas!" she sobb'd, — "and yet be gone,
And speed thee forth, like Duncan's son!"
One look he cast upon the bier,   420
Dash'd from his eye the gathering tear,
Breathed deep to clear his labouring breast,
And toss'd aloft his bonnet crest,
Then, like the high-bred colt, when, freed,

First he essays his fire and speed,   425
He vanish'd, and o'er moor and moss
Sped forward with the Fiery Cross.
Suspended was the widow's tear,
While yet his footsteps she could hear;
And when she mark'd the henchman's eye   430
Wet with unwonted sympathy,
"Kinsman," she said, "his race is run,
That should have sped thine errand on;
The oak has fall'n, — the sapling bough
Is all Duncraggan's shelter now.[1]   435
Yet trust I well, his duty done,
The orphan's God will guard my son. —
And you, in many a danger true,
At Duncan's hest[2] your blades that drew,
To arms, and guard that orphan's head!   440
Let babes and women wail the dead."
Then weapon-clang, and martial call,
Resounded through the funeral hall,
While from the walls the attendant band
Snatch'd sword and targe,[3] with hurried hand; 445
And short and flitting energy
Glanced from the mourner's sunken eye,
As if the sounds to warrior dear,
Might rouse her Duncan from his bier.
But faded soon that borrow'd force;   450
Grief claim'd his right, and tears their course.

XIX

Ben Ledi saw the Cross of Fire,
It glanced like lightning up Strath-Ire.
O'er dale and hill the summons flew,
Nor rest nor pause young Angus knew;   455

[1] Duncan's son, Angus, is now the protector of Duncraggan.
[2] behest, command   [3] shield

The tear that gather'd in his eye
He left the mountain breeze to dry;
Until, where Teith's young waters roll,
Betwixt him and a wooded knoll,
That graced the sable strath with green,   460
The chapel of St. Bride [1] was seen.
Swoln was the stream, remote the bridge,
But Angus paused not on the edge;
Though the dark waves danced dizzily,
Though reel'd his sympathetic eye,   465
He dash'd amid the torrent's roar:
His right hand high the crosslet bore,
His left the pole-axe grasp'd, to guide
And stay his footing in the tide.
He stumbled twice — the foam splash'd high;   470
With hoarser swell the stream raced by;
And had he fall'n, — for ever there,
Farewell Duncraggan's orphan heir!
But still, as if in parting life,
Firmer he grasp'd the Cross of strife,   475
Until the opposing bank he gain'd,
And up the chapel pathway strain'd.

XX

A blithesome rout, that morning tide,
Had sought the chapel of St. Bride.
Her troth [2] Tombea's Mary gave   480
To Norman, heir of Armandave. [3]
And, issuing from the Gothic arch,
The bridal now resumed their march.
In rude, but glad procession, came
Bonneted sire and coif-clad [4] dame;   485

[1] near Strath-Ire
[2] bethrothal
[3] near Strath-Ire
[4] caps that the women wore as distinguished from the maiden's snood

And plaided youth, with jest and jeer,
Which snooded maiden would not hear:
And children, that, unwitting why,[1]
Lent the gay shout their shrilly cry;
And minstrels, that in measures vied   490
Before the young and bonny bride,
Whose downcast eye and cheek disclose
The tear and blush of morning rose.
With virgin step, and bashful hand,
She held the 'kerchief's snowy band;   495
The gallant bridegroom, by her side,
Beheld his prize with victor's pride,
And the glad mother in her ear
Was closely whispering word of cheer.

XXI

Who meets them at the churchyard gate?   500
The messenger of fear and fate!
Haste in his hurried accent lies,
And grief is swimming in his eyes.
All dripping from the recent flood,
Panting and travel-soil'd he stood,   505
The fatal sign of fire and sword
Held forth, and spoke the appointed word:
"The muster-place is Lanrick mead;
Speed forth the signal! Norman,[2] speed!"
And must he change so soon the hand,   510
Just link'd to his by holy band,
For the fell Cross of blood and brand?
And must the day, so blithe that rose,
And promised rapture in the close,
Before its setting hour, divide   515
The bridegroom from the plighted bride?

---

[1] not knowing why
[2] Norman now carries the signal in place of Angus.

O fatal doom! — it must! it must!
Clan-Alpine's cause, her Chieftain's trust,
Her summons dread, brook no delay;
Stretch to the race — away! away!   520

XXII

Yet slow he laid his plaid aside,
And, lingering, eyed his lovely bride,
Until he saw the starting tear
Speak woe he might not stop to cheer;
Then, trusting not a second look,   525
In haste he sped him up the brook,
Nor backward glanced, till on the heath
Where Lubnaig's lake supplies the Teith.
— What in the racer's bosom stirr'd?
The sickening pang of hope deferr'd,   530
And memory, with a torturing train
Of all his morning visions vain.
Mingled with love's impatience, came
The manly thirst for martial fame;
The stormy joy of mountaineers,   535
Ere yet they rush upon the spears;
And zeal for Clan and Chieftain burning,
And hope, from well-fought field returning,
With war's red honours on his crest,
To clasp his Mary to his breast.   540
Stung by such thoughts, o'er bank and brae,
Like fire from flint he glanced away,
While high resolve, and feeling strong,
Burst into voluntary song.

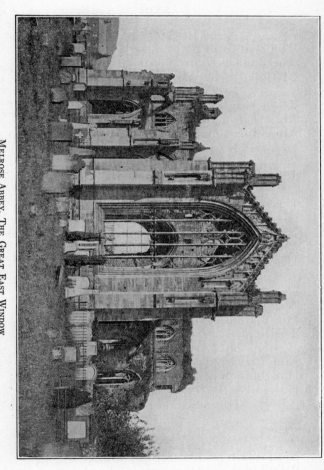

MELROSE ABBEY, THE GREAT EAST WINDOW

The heart of Robert Bruce was buried beneath the high altar. Photo by Ewing Galloway.

XXIII

Song

The heath this night must be my bed, 545
The bracken [1] curtain for my head,
My lullaby the warder's tread,
   Far, far, from love and thee, **Mary**;
To-morrow eve, more stilly laid,
My couch may be my bloody plaid, 550
My vesper song,[2] thy wail, sweet maid!
   It will not waken me, Mary!

I may not, dare not, fancy now
The grief that clouds thy lovely brow,
I dare not think upon thy vow, 555
   And all it promised me, Mary.
No fond regret must Norman know;
When bursts Clan-Alpine on the foe,
His heart must be like bended bow,
   His foot like arrow free, Mary. 560

A time will come with feeling fraught,
For, if I fall in battle fought,
Thy hapless [3] lover's dying thought
   Shall be a thought on thee, **Mary**.
And if return'd from conquer'd foes, 565
How blithely will the evening close,
How sweet the linnet sing repose,
   To my young bride and me, Mary!

XXIV

Not faster o'er thy heathery braes,
Balquidder, speeds the midnight blaze, 570

---

[1] "brakes," ferns [2] evening song [3] unfortunate

Rushing, in conflagration strong,
Thy deep ravines and dells along,
Wrapping thy cliffs in purple glow,
And reddening the dark lakes below;
Nor faster speeds it, nor so far,   575
As o'er thy heaths the voice of war.
The signal roused to martial coil,
The sullen margin of Loch Voil,
Waked still Loch Doine, and to the source
Alarm'd, Balvaig, thy swampy course;   580
Thence southward turn'd its rapid road,
Adown Strath-Gartney's valley broad,
Till rose in arms each man might claim [1]
A portion in Clan-Alpine's name,
From the grey sire, whose trembling hand   585
Could hardly buckle on his brand,
To the raw boy, whose shaft and bow
Were yet scarce terror to the crow.
Each valley, each sequester'd glen,
Muster'd its little horde of men,   590
That met as torrents from the height
In Highland dales their streams unite,
Still gathering, as they pour along,
A voice more loud, a tide more strong,
Till at the rendezvous [2] they stood   595
By hundreds prompt for blows and blood,
Each train'd to arms since life began,
Owning no tie but to his clan,
No oath, but by his chieftain's hand,
No law, but Roderick Dhu's command.   600

XXV

That summer morn had Roderick Dhu
Survey'd the skirts of Ben Venue,

[1] *who* could claim   [2] meeting place

And sent his scouts o'er hill and heath,
To view the frontiers of Menteith.
All backward came with news of truce;   605
Still lay each martial Graeme [1] and Bruce,[1]
In Rednoch courts no horsemen wait,
No banner waved on Cardross gate,
On Duchray's towers no beacon shone,[2]
Nor scared the herons from Loch Con;   610
All seem'd at peace. — Now wot ye why
The Chieftain, with such anxious eye,
Ere to the muster he repair,
This western frontier scann'd with care? —
In Ben Venue's most darksome cleft,   615
A fair, though cruel, pledge was left;
For Douglas, to his promise true,
That morning from the isle withdrew,
And in a deep sequester'd dell
Had sought a low and lonely cell.   620
By many a bard, in Celtic tongue,
Has Coir-nan-Uriskin [3] been sung;
A softer name the Saxons gave,
And call'd the grot the Goblin-cave.

XXVI

It was a wild and strange retreat,   625
As e'er was trod by outlaw's feet.
The dell, upon the mountain's crest,
Yawn'd like a gash on warrior's breast;
Its trench had staid full many a rock,
Hurl'd by primeval earthquake shock   630
From Ben Venue's grey summit wild,
And here, in random ruin piled,

1 strong and powerful Lowland families
2 the castles he passed
3 "Den of the Wild or Shaggy Men"

They frown'd incumbent o'er the spot,
And form'd the rugged silvan grot.
The oak and birch, with mingled shade,   635
At noontide there a twilight made,
Unless when short and sudden shone
Some straggling beam on cliff or stone,
With such a glimpse as prophet's eye
Gains on thy depth, Futurity.   640
No murmur waked the solemn still,[1]
Save tinkling of a fountain rill;
But when the wind chafed with the lake,
A sullen sound would upward break,
With dashing hollow voice, that spoke   645
The incessant war of wave and rock.
Suspended cliffs, with hideous sway,
Seem'd nodding o'er the cavern grey.
From such a den the wolf had sprung,
In such the wild-cat leaves her young;   650
Yet Douglas and his daughter fair
Sought for a space their safety there.
Grey Superstition's whisper dread
Debarr'd the spot to vulgar tread;
For there, she said, did fays resort,   655
And satyrs[2] hold their silvan court,
By moonlight tread their mystic maze,
And blast the rash beholder's gaze.

XXVII

Now eve, with western shadows long,
Floated on Katrine bright and strong,   660
When Roderick, with a chosen few,
Repass'd the heights of Ben Venue.

[1] For the sake of the rhyme the adjective is used as subject.
[2] silvan deities of Greek mythology. Their heads and bodies were like a man's; their legs those of a goat.

Above the Goblin-cave they go,
Through the wild pass of Beal-nam-bo:
The prompt retainers speed before,   665
To launch the shallop from the shore,
For 'cross Loch Katrine lies his way
To view the passes of Achray,
And place his clansmen in array.
Yet lags the Chief in musing mind,   670
Unwonted sight, his men behind.
A single page, to bear his sword,
Alone attended on his lord;
The rest their way through thickets break,
And soon await him by the lake.   675
It was a fair and gallant sight,
To view them from the neighbouring height,
By the low-levell'd sunbeam's light!
For strength and stature, from the clan
Each warrior was a chosen man,   680
As even afar might well be seen,
By their proud step and martial mien.
Their feathers dance, their tartans float,
Their targets gleam, as by the boat
A wild and warlike group they stand,   685
That well became such mountain-strand.

XXVIII

Their Chief, with step reluctant, still
Was lingering on the craggy hill,
Hard by where turn'd apart the road
To Douglas's obscure abode.   690
It was but with that dawning morn,
That Roderick Dhu had proudly sworn
To drown his love in war's wild roar,
Nor think of Ellen Douglas more;

But he who stems [1] a stream with sand,   695
And fetters flame with flaxen band,
Has yet a harder task to prove —
By firm resolve to conquer love!
Eve finds the Chief, like restless ghost,
Still hovering near his treasure lost;   700
For though his haughty heart deny
A parting meeting to his eye,
Still fondly strains his anxious ear,
The accents of her voice to hear,
And inly [2] did he curse the breeze   705
That waked to sound the rustling trees.
But hark! what mingles in the strain?
It is the harp of Allan-bane,
That wakes its measure slow and high,
Attuned to sacred minstrelsy.   710
What melting voice attends the strings?
'Tis Ellen, or an angel, sings.

XXIX

Hymn to the Virgin

Ave Maria! [3] maiden mild!
    Listen to a maiden's prayer!
Thou canst hear though from the wild,   715
    Thou canst save amid despair.
Safe may we sleep beneath thy care,
    Though banish'd, outcast, and reviled —
Maiden! hear a maiden's prayer;
    Mother, hear a suppliant child!   720
                    Ave Maria!

---

[1] checks
[2] secretly
[3] "Hail Mary," the beginning of the prayer to the Virgin

Ave Maria! undefiled!
 The flinty couch we now must share
Shall seem with down of eider [1] piled,
 If thy protection hover there.
The murky cavern's heavy air   725
 Shall breathe of balm if thou hast smiled;
Then, Maiden! hear a maiden's prayer;
 Mother, list a suppliant child!
       Ave Maria!

Ave Maria! stainless styled!
 Foul demons of the earth and air,   730
From this their wonted haunt exiled,
 Shall flee before thy presence fair.
We bow us to our lot of care,
 Beneath thy guidance reconciled;
Hear for a maid a maiden's prayer,   735
 And for a father hear a child!
       Ave Maria!

XXX

Died on the harp the closing hymn —
Unmoved in attitude and limb,
As list'ning still, Clan-Alpine's lord
Stood leaning on his heavy sword,   740
Until the page, with humble sign,
Twice pointed to the sun's decline.
Then while his plaid he round him cast,
"It is the last time — 'tis the last,"
He muttered thrice, — "the last time e'er 745
That angel voice shall Roderick hear!"
It was a goading thought — his stride
Hied hastier down the mountain side;

---

[1] the soft feathers of the eider duck

Sullen he flung him in the boat,
And instant 'cross the lake it shot.   750
They landed in that silvery bay,
And eastward held their hasty way,
Till, with the latest beams of light,
The band arrived on Lanrick height,[1]
Where muster'd, in the vale below,   755
Clan-Alpine's men in martial show.

XXXI

A various scene the clansmen made,
Some sate, some stood, some slowly stray'd;
But most with mantles folded round,
Were couch'd to rest upon the ground,   760
Scarce to be known by curious eye,
From the deep heather where they lie,
So well was match'd the tartan screen
With heath-bell dark and brackens green,
Unless where, here and there, a blade,   765
Or lance's point, a glimmer made,
Like glow-worm twinkling through the shade,
But when, advancing through the gloom,
They saw the Chieftain's eagle plume,
Their shout of welcome, shrill and wide,   770
Shook the steep mountain's steady side.
Thrice it arose, and lake and fell
Three times return'd the martial yell;
It died upon Bochastle's plain,[2]
And Silence claim'd her evening reign.   775

[1] overlooking Lanrick mead
[2] somewhat to the eastward

CANTO FOURTH

THE PROPHECY

I

"THE rose is fairest when 'tis budding new,
  And hope is brightest when it dawns from fears;
The rose is sweetest wash'd with morning dew,
  And love is loveliest when embalm'd in tears.
  O wilding [1] rose, whom fancy thus endears,   5
I bid your blossoms in my bonnet wave,
  Emblem of hope and love through future years!" —
Thus spoke young Norman, heir of Armandave,
What time the sun arose on Vennachar's broad wave.

II

Such fond conceit,[2] half said, half sung,   10
Love prompted to the bridegroom's tongue.
All while he stripp'd the wild-rose spray,
His axe and bow beside him lay,
For on a pass 'twixt lake and wood,
A wakeful sentinel he stood.   15
Hark! — on the rock a footstep rung,
And instant to his arms he sprung.
"Stand, or thou diest! — What, Malise? — soon
Art thou return'd from Braes of Doune.
By thy keen step and glance I know,   20
Thou bring'st us tidings of the foe." —
(For while the Fiery Cross hied on,
On distant scout had Malise gone.)
"Where sleeps the Chief?" the henchman said.
"Apart, in yonder misty glade;   25
To his lone couch I'll be your guide." —
Then call'd a slumberer by his side,

---

[1] wildings used only in poetry   [2] thought

And stirr'd him with his slacken'd bow —
"Up, up, Glentarkin! rouse thee, ho!
We seek the Chieftain; on the track,   30
Keep eagle watch till I come back."

III

Together up the pass they sped:
"What of the foeman?" Norman said. —
"Varying reports from near and far;
This certain, — that a band of war   35
Has for two days been ready boune,[1]
At prompt command, to march from Doune; [2]
King James, the while, with princely powers,
Holds revelry in Stirling towers.
Soon will this dark and gathering cloud   40
Speak on our glens in thunder loud.
Inured to bide such bitter bout,[3]
The warrior's plaid may bear it out;
But, Norman, how wilt thou provide
A shelter for thy bonny bride?" —   45
"What! know ye not that Roderick's care
To the lone isle hath caused repair [4]
Each maid and matron of the clan,
And every child and aged man
Unfit for arms; and given his charge,   50
Nor skiff nor shallop, boat nor barge,
Upon these lakes shall float at large,
But all beside the islet moor,
That such dear pledge may rest secure?" —

IV

"'Tis well advised [5] — the Chieftain's plan   55
Bespeaks the father of his clan.

---

[1] ready or prepared   [2] an old castle on the Teith
[3] bide = endure; bout = luck   [4] to go (for safety)   [5] well planned

But wherefore sleeps Sir Roderick Dhu
Apart from all his followers true?" —
"It is, because last evening-tide
Brian an augury hath tried,   60
Of that dread kind which must not be
Unless in dread extremity,
The Taghairm [1] call'd; by which, afar,
Our sires foresaw the events of war.
Duncraggan's milk-white bull they slew."   65

MALISE

"Ah! Well the gallant brute I knew
The choicest of the prey we had,
When swept our merry-men Gallangad.[2]
His hide was snow, his horns were dark,
His red eye glow'd like fiery spark;   70
So fierce, so tameless, and so fleet,
Sore did he cumber [3] our retreat,
And kept our stoutest kernes [4] in awe,
Even at the pass of Beal 'maha.
But steep and flinty was the road,   75
And sharp the hurrying pikeman's goad,
And when we came to Dennan's Row,[5]
A child might scathless [6] stroke his brow." —

[1] "The Highlanders, like all rude people, had various superstitious modes of inquiring into futurity. One of the most noted was the *Taghairm* mentioned in the text. A person was wrapped up in the skin of a newly-slain bullock, and deposited beside a waterfall, or at the bottom of a precipice, or in some other strange, wild, and unusual situation, where the scenery around him suggested nothing but objects of horror. In this situation he revolved in his mind the question proposed, and whatever was impressed upon him by his exalted imagination passed for the inspiration of the disembodied spirits who haunt the desolate recesses." Scott.

[2] Gallangad, a place south of Loch Lomond where a Highland "cattle-drive" took place

[3] encumber

[4] foot soldiers

[5] now called Rowardennan, where tourists begin the ascent of Ben Lomond

[6] fearless

V
NORMAN

"That bull was slain: his reeking hide
They stretch'd the cataract beside,   80
Whose waters their wild tumult toss
Adown the black and craggy boss [1]
Of that huge cliff, whose ample verge
Tradition calls the Hero's Targe. [2]
Couch'd on a shelve beneath its brink,   85
Close where the thundering torrents sink,
Rocking beneath their headlong sway,
And drizzled by the ceaseless spray,
Midst groan of rock, and roar of stream,
The wizard waits prophetic dream.   90
Nor distant rests the Chief; — but hush!
See, gliding slow through mist and bush,
The hermit gains yon rock, and stands
To gaze upon our slumbering bands.
Seems he not, Malise, like a ghost,   95
That hovers o'er a slaughter'd host?
Or raven on the blasted oak,
That, watching while the deer is broke, [3]
His morsel claims with sullen croak?"

MALISE

— "Peace! peace! to other than to me,   100
Thy words were evil augury;
But still I hold Sir Roderick's blade
Clan-Alpine's omen and her aid,
Not aught that, glean'd from heaven or hell,
Yon fiend-begotten [4] Monk can tell.   105
The Chieftain joins him, see — and now,
Together they descend the brow."

---

[1] protuberance, knob   [2] a rock in the Forest of Glenfinlas
[3] cut up, quartered   [4] an allusion to the mysterious birth of Brian

VI

And, as they came, with Alpine's Lord
The Hermit Monk held solemn word: —
"Roderick! it is a fearful strife,   110
For man endow'd with mortal life,
Whose shroud of sentient [1] clay can still
Feel feverish pang and fainting chill.
Whose eye can stare in stony trance,
Whose hair can rouse [2] like warrior's lance, —   115
'Tis hard for such to view, unfurl'd,
The curtain of the future world.
Yet, witness every quaking limb,
My sunken pulse, my eyeballs dim,
My soul with harrowing anguish torn, —   120
This for my Chieftain have I borne! —
The shapes that sought my fearful couch,
A human tongue may ne'er avouch,[3]
No mortal man, — save he, who, bred
Between the living and the dead,   125
Is gifted beyond nature's law, —
Had e'er survived to say he saw.
At length the fatal answer came,
In characters of living flame!
Not spoke in word, nor blazed [4] in scroll,   130
But borne and branded on my soul; —
Which spills the foremost foeman's life,
That party conquers in the strife." [5]

VII

"Thanks, Brian, for thy zeal and care!
Good is thine augury, and fair.   135

---

[1] man's feeling flesh, his body   [2] stand on end   [3] vouch for   [4] emblazoned
[5] "Though this be in the text described as the response of the Taghairm, or
Oracle of the Hide, it was of itself an augury frequently attended to. The fate of the
battle was often anticipated, in the imagination of the combatants, by observing
which party shed first blood." Scott.

Clan-Alpine ne'er in battle stood,
But first our broadswords tasted blood.
A surer victim still I know,
Self-offer'd to the auspicious blow:
A spy has sought my land [1] this morn, —   140
No eve shall witness his return!
My followers guard each pass's mouth,
To east, to westward, and to south;
Red Murdoch,[2] bribed to be his guide,
Has charge to lead his steps aside,   145
Till, in deep path or dingle brown,
He light on those shall bring him down.
— But see, who comes his news to show!
Malise! what tidings of the foe?" —

VIII

"At Doune, o'er many a spear and glaive [3]   150
Two Barons proud their banners wave.
I saw the Moray's silver star,
And mark'd the sable pale of Mar." — [4]
"By Alpine's soul, high tidings those!
I love to hear of worthy foes.   155
When move they on?" — "To-morrow's noon
Will see them here for battle boune." —
"Then shall it see a meeting stern! —
But, for the place — say, couldst thou learn
Nought of the friendly clans of Earn?   160
Strengthen'd by them, we well might bide
The battle on Ben Ledi's side.
Thou couldst not? — well! Clan-Alpine's men
Shall man the Trossachs' shaggy glen;

[1] James Fitz-James, the Knight of Snowdoun
[2] a desperate warrior
[3] sword
[4] the coats-of-arms of two noted families. Moray and Mar assisted in the
leadership of the forces of Fitz-James.

Within Loch Katrine's gorge we'll fight,　165
All in our maids' and matrons' sight,
Each for his hearth and household fire,
Father for child, and son for sire, —
Lover for maid beloved! — But why —
Is it the breeze affects mine eye?　170
Or dost thou come, ill omen'd tear!
A messenger of doubt and fear?
No! sooner may the Saxon lance
Unfix Ben Ledi from his stance,[1]
Than doubt or terror can pierce through　175
The unyielding heart of Roderick Dhu!
'Tis stubborn as his trusty targe. —
Each to his post — all know their charge."
The pibroch sounds, the bands advance,
The broadswords gleam, the banners dance,　180
Obedient to the Chieftain's glance.
— I turn me from the martial roar,
And seek Coir-Uriskin once more.

IX

Where is the Douglas? — he is gone;
And Ellen sits on the grey stone　185
Fast by the cave, and makes her moan;
While vainly Allan's words of cheer
Are pour'd on her unheeding ear. —
"He will return — Dear lady, trust! —
With joy return; — he will — he must.　190
Well was it time to seek, afar,
Some refuge from impending war,
When e'en Clan-Alpine's rugged swarm
Are cow'd by the approaching storm.
I saw their boats with many a light,　195
Floating the live-long yesternight,

---

[1] station, foundation

Shifting like flashes darted forth
By the red streamers of the north; [1]
I mark'd at morn how close they ride,
Thick moor'd by the lone islet's side,   200
Like wild-ducks couching in the fen,
When stoops the hawk upon the glen.
Since this rude race dare not abide
The peril on the mainland side,
Shall not thy noble father's care   205
Some safe retreat for thee prepare?"

X

ELLEN

"No, Allan, no! Pretext so kind
My wakeful terrors could not blind.
When in such tender tone, yet grave,
Douglas a parting blessing gave,   210
The tear that glisten'd in his eye
Drown'd not his purpose fix'd on high.
My soul, though feminine and weak,
Can image his; e'en as the lake,
Itself disturb'd by slightest stroke,   215
Reflects the invulnerable rock.
He hears report of battle rife,
He deems himself the cause of strife.
I saw him redden, when the theme
Turn'd, Allan, on thine idle dream   220
Of Malcolm Graeme in fetters bound,
Which I, thou saidst, about him wound.
Think'st thou he trow'd thine omen aught?
Oh, no! 'twas apprehensive thought
For the kind youth, — for Roderick too —   225
(Let me be just) that friend so true;

[1] Aurora Borealis, Northern Lights

In danger both, and in our cause!
Minstrel, the Douglas dare not pause.
Why else that solemn warning given,
'If not on earth, we meet in heaven!'   230
Why else, to Cambus-Kenneth's fane [1]
If eve return him not again,
Am I to hie, and make me known?
Alas! he goes to Scotland's throne,
Buys his friend's safety with his own; —   235
He goes to do — what I had done,
Had Douglas' daughter been his son!" —

XI

"Nay, lovely Ellen! — dearest, nay!
If aught should his return delay,
He only named yon holy fane   240
As fitting place to meet again.
Be sure he's safe; and for the Graeme, —
Heaven's blessing on his gallant name! —
My vision'd sight may yet prove true,
Nor bode of [2] ill to him or you.   245
When did my gifted dream beguile? [3]
Think of the stranger at the isle,
And think upon the harpings slow,
That presaged [4] this approaching woe!
Sooth [5] was my prophecy of fear;   250
Believe it when it augurs cheer.
Would we had left this dismal spot!
Ill luck still haunts a fairy grot.
Of such a wondrous tale I know —
Dear lady, change that look of woe,   255
My harp was wont thy grief to cheer."

---

[1] Cambus-Kenneth Abbey stood near the Forth River near Stirling
[2] forebode   [3] deceive   [4] foretold   [5] true

ELLEN

"Well, be it as thou wilt; I hear,
But cannot stop the bursting tear."
The Minstrel tried his simple art,
But distant far was Ellen's heart.   260

XII

Ballad — Alice Brand

Merry it is in the good greenwood,
 When the mavis and merle [1] are singing,
When the deer sweeps by, and the hounds are in
  cry,
 And the hunter's horn is ringing.

"O Alice Brand, my native land   265
 Is lost for love of you;
And we must hold by wood and wold, [2]
 As outlaws wont to do.

"O Alice, 'twas all for thy locks so bright,
 And 'twas all for thine eyes so blue,   270
That on the night of our luckless flight,
 Thy brother bold I slew.

"Now must I teach to hew the beech
 The hand that held the glaive, [3]
For leaves to spread our lowly bed,   275
 And stakes to fence our cave.

"And for vest of pall, [4] thy fingers small,
 That wont on harp to stray,
A cloak must shear from the slaughter'd deer,
 To keep the cold away." —   280

---

[1] thrush and blackbird   [2] open country   [3] broadsword
[4] rich cloth of which mantles were made

"O Richard! if my brother died,
   'Twas but a fatal chance;
For darkling [1] was the battle tried,
   And fortune sped the lance.

"If pall and vair [2] no more I wear,   285
   Nor thou the crimson sheen,[3]
As warm, we'll say, is the russet grey,[4]
   As gay the forest-green.[5]

"And, Richard, if our lot be hard,
   And lost thy native land,   290
Still Alice has her own Richard,
   And he his Alice Brand."

XIII

Ballad Continued

'Tis merry, 'tis merry, in good greenwood,
   So blithe Lady Alice is singing;
On the beech's pride, and oak's brown side,   295
   Lord Richard's axe is ringing.

Up spoke the moody Elfin King,
   Who wonn'd [6] within the hill, —
Like wind in the porch of a ruin'd church,
   His voice was ghostly shrill.   300

"Why sounds yon stroke on beech and oak,
   Our moonlight circle's screen?
Or who comes here to chase the deer,
   Beloved of our Elfin Queen?

[1] a poetical word, "in the dark"   [2] squirrel's fur   [3] bright
[4] coarse homespun cloth   [5] a hunter's clothing   [6] dwelt

Or who may dare on wold to wear   305
    The fairies' fatal green? [1]

"Up, Urgan,[2] up! to yon mortal hie,
    For thou wert christen'd man; [3]
For cross or sign thou wilt not fly,
    For mutter'd word or ban.   310

"Lay on him the curse of the wither'd heart,
    The curse of the sleepless eye;
Till he wish and pray that his life would part,[4]
    Nor yet find leave to die."

XIV

Ballad Continued

'Tis merry, 'tis merry, in good greenwood,   315
    Though the birds have still'd their singing;
The evening blaze doth Alice raise,
    And Richard is fagots bringing.

Up Urgan starts, that hideous dwarf,
    Before Lord Richard stands,   320
And, as he cross'd and bless'd himself,
"I fear not sign," quoth the grisly elf,
    "That is made with bloody hands."

But out then spoke she, Alice Brand,
    That woman void of fear, —   325
"And if there's blood upon his hand,
    'Tis but the blood of deer." —

[1] Since green was the color worn by the elves or gnomes, many people believe misfortune will come to those who wear it.
[2] a knight who became a dwarf and lived with the elves
[3] Demons and fairies were deathly afraid of the sign of the cross. Having been baptized, Urgan had nothing to fear from the sign.   [4] depart

"Now loud thou liest, thou bold of mood!
    It cleaves unto his hand,
The stain of thine own kindly [1] blood,   330
    The blood of Ethert Brand."

Then forward stepp'd she, Alice Brand,
    And made the holy sign, —
"And if there's blood on Richard's hand,
    A spotless hand is mine.   335

"And I conjure thee, Demon elf,
    By Him whom Demons fear,
To show us whence thou art thyself,
    And what thine errand here?" —

XV

Ballad Continued

"'Tis merry, 'tis merry, in Fairy-land   340
    When fairy birds are singing,
When the court doth ride by their monarch's side
    With bit and bridle ringing:

"And gaily shines the Fairy-land —
    But all is glistening show,   345
Like the idle gleam that December's beam
    Can dart on ice and snow.

"And fading, like that varied gleam,
    Is our inconstant shape, [2]
Who now like knight and lady seem,   350
    And now like dwarf and ape.

---

[1] kindred
[2] In the land of the elfs, people assumed different sizes.

"It was between the night and day,
　　When the Fairy King has power,
That I sunk down in a sinful fray,
And, 'twixt life and death, was snatch'd away　　355
　　To the joyless Elfin bower.

"But wist I of a woman bold,
　　Who thrice my brow durst sign,[1]
I might regain my mortal mould,
　　As fair a form as thine."　　360

She cross'd him once — she cross'd him twice —
　　That lady was so brave;
The fouler grew his goblin hue,
　　The darker grew the cave.

She cross'd him thrice, that lady bold;　　365
　　He rose beneath her hand
The fairest knight on Scottish mould,
　　Her brother, Ethert Brand!

Merry it is in good greenwood,
　　When the mavis and merle are singing,　　370
But merrier were they in Dunfermline [2] grey,
　　When all the bells were ringing.

XVI

Just as the minstrel sounds were staid,
A stranger climb'd the steepy glade·
His martial step, his stately mien,　　375
His hunting suit of Lincoln green,

---

[1] dared make the sign of the cross upon his brow
[2] A town seventeen miles northwest from Edinburgh where numerous kings were buried in the old abbey. Robert Bruce was the last to be buried there.

His eagle glance, remembrance claims —
'Tis Snowdoun's Knight, 'tis James Fitz-James.
Ellen beheld as in a dream,
Then, starting, scarce suppress'd a scream.   380
"O stranger! in such hour of fear,
What evil hap [1] has brought thee here?"—
"An evil hap how can it be,
That bids me look again on thee?
By promise bound, my former guide [2]   385
Met me betimes this morning tide,
And marshall'd, over bank and bourne,[3]
The happy path of my return." —
"The happy path! — what! said he nought
Of war, of battle to be fought,   390
Of guarded pass?" — "No, by my faith!
Nor saw I aught could augur scathe." — [4]
"O haste thee, Allan, to the kern,
— Yonder his tartans I discern;
Learn thou his purpose, and conjure [5]   395
That he will guide the stranger sure! —
What prompted thee, unhappy man?
The meanest serf in Roderick's clan
Had not been bribed [6] by love or fear,
Unknown to him to guide thee here." —   400

XVII

"Sweet Ellen, dear my life must be
Since it is worthy care from thee;
Yet life I hold but idle breath,
When love or honour's weigh'd with death.
Then let me profit by my chance,   405
And speak my purpose bold at once.

---

[1] chance   [2] the leader, Red Murdoch   [3] boundary
[4] harm   [5] the word *him* is understood: hence — urge him.
[6] would not have been bribed

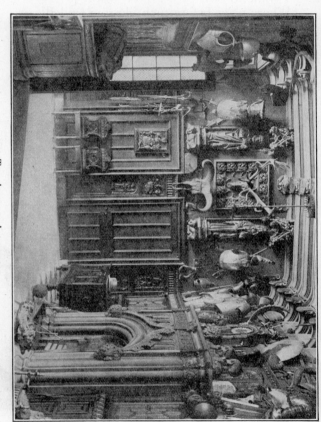

THE ARMORY, ABBOTSFORD

On the walls are a casque, several hauberks, and a targe. Photo by Ewing Galloway.

I come to bear thee from a wild,
Where ne'er before such blossom smiled;
By this soft hand to lead thee far
From frantic scenes of feud and war.   410
Near Bochastle my horses wait;
They bear us soon to Stirling gate.
I'll place thee in a lovely bower,
I'll guard thee like a tender flower" —
"O! hush, Sir Knight! 'twere female art,[1]   415
To say I do not read thy heart;
Too much, before, my selfish ear
Was idly soothed my praise to hear.
That fatal bait hath lured thee back,
In deathful hour, o'er dangerous track;   420
And how, O how, can I atone
The wreck my vanity brought on! —
One way remains — I'll tell him all —
Yes! struggling bosom, forth it shall![2]
Thou, whose light folly bears the blame,   425
Buy thine own pardon with thy shame!
But first — my father is a man
Outlaw'd and exiled, under ban;
The price of blood is on his head,
With me 'twere infamy to wed. —   430
Still wouldst thou speak? — then hear the truth!
Fitz-James, there is a noble youth, —
If yet he is![3] — exposed for me
And mine to dread extremity —
Thou hast the secret of my heart;   435
Forgive, be generous, and depart!"

XVIII

Fitz-James knew every wily train[4]
A lady's fickle heart to gain,

---

[1] affectation   [2] it shall be said.   [3] if he is still living   [4] clever device, lure

But here he knew and felt them vain.
There shot no glance from Ellen's eye,   440
To give her steadfast speech the lie;
In maiden confidence she stood,
Though mantled in her cheek the blood,
And told her love with such a sigh
Of deep and hopeless agony,   445
As death had seal'd her Malcolm's doom,
And she sat sorrowing on his tomb.
Hope vanish'd from Fitz-James's eye,
But not with hope fled sympathy.
He proffer'd to attend her side,   450
As brother would a sister guide. —
"O! little know'st thou Roderick's heart!
Safer for both we go apart.
O haste thee, and from Allan learn,
If thou may'st trust yon wily kern." [1]   455
With hand upon his forehead laid,
The conflict of his mind to shade,
A parting step or two he made;
Then, as some thought had cross'd his brain,
He paused, and turn'd, and came again.   460

XIX

"Hear, lady, yet, a parting word! —
It chanced in fight that my poor sword
Preserved the life of Scotland's lord.
This ring the grateful Monarch gave,
And bade, when I had boon to crave,   465
To bring it back, and boldly claim
The recompense that I would name.
Ellen, I am no courtly lord,
But one who lives by lance and sword,
Whose castle is his helm and shield,   470

---

[1] deceitful soldier

His lordship [1] the embattled field. [2]
What from a prince can I demand,
Who neither reck of [3] state nor land?
Ellen, thy hand — the ring is thine;
Each guard and usher knows the sign.   475
Seek thou the king without delay;
This signet [4] shall secure thy way;
And claim thy suit, [5] whate'er it be,
As ransom of his pledge to me."
He placed the golden circlet on,   480
Paused — kiss'd her hand — and then was gone.
The aged Minstrel stood aghast,
So hastily Fitz-James shot past.
He join'd his guide, and wending down
The ridges of the mountain brown,   485
Across the stream they took their way,
That joins Loch Katrine to Achray.

XX

All in the Trossachs' glen was still,
Noontide was sleeping on the hill:
Sudden his guide whoop'd loud and high —   490
"Murdoch! was that a signal cry?" —
He stammer'd forth — "I shout to scare
Yon raven from his dainty fare."
He look'd — he knew the raven's prey,
His own brave steed: — "Ah! gallant grey!   495
For thee — for me, perchance — 'twere well
We ne'er had seen the Trossachs' dell. —
Murdoch, move first [6] — but silently;
Whistle or whoop, and thou shalt die!"
Jealous and sullen on they fared, [7]   500
Each silent, each upon his guard.

[1] lordly estate   [2] battle field   [3] care for   [4] ring
[5] secure your request.   The ring usually commanded the same attention from officials as a king's passport.   [6] go on   [7] went

XXI

Now wound the path its dizzy ledge
Around a precipice's edge,
When lo! a wasted female form,
Blighted by wrath of sun and storm,   505
In tatter'd weeds [1] and wild array,
Stood on a cliff beside the way,
And glancing round her restless eye,
Upon the wood, the rock, the sky,
Seem'd nought to mark, yet all to spy.   510
Her brow was wreath'd with gaudy broom; [2]
With gesture wild she waved a plume
Of feathers, which the eagles fling
To crag and cliff from dusky wing;
Such spoils her desperate step had sought,   515
Where scarce was footing for the goat.
The tartan plaid she first descried,
And shriek'd till all the rocks replied;
As loud she laugh'd when near they drew,
For then the Lowland garb she knew;   520
And then her hands she wildly wrung,
And then she wept, and then she sung —
She sung! — the voice, in better time, [3]
Perchance to harp or lute might chime;
And now, though strain'd and roughen'd, still   525
Rung wildly sweet to dale and hill.

XXII

Song

They bid me sleep, they bid me pray,
    They say my brain is warp'd and wrung —
I cannot sleep on Highland brae,
    I cannot pray in Highland tongue.   530

[1] clothes   [2] a plant with bright yellow blossoms   [3] days

But were I now where Allan glides,
Or heard my native Devan's tides,[1]
So sweetly would I rest, and pray
That Heaven would close my wintry day!

'Twas thus my hair they bade me braid,   535
   They made me to the church repair;
It was my bridal morn they said,
   And my truelove would meet me there.
But woe betide the cruel guile,
That drown'd in blood the morning smile!   540
And woe betide the fairy dream!
I only waked to sob and scream.

XXIII

"Who is this maid? what means her lay?
She hovers o'er the hollow way,
And flutters wide her mantle grey,   545
As the lone heron spreads his wing,
By twilight, o'er a haunted spring."
"'Tis Blanche of Devan," Murdoch said
"A crazed and captive Lowland maid,
Ta'en on the morn she was a bride,   550
When Roderick foray'd Devan side.
The gay bridegroom resistance made,
And felt our Chief's unconquer'd blade.
I marvel she is now at large,
But oft she 'scapes from Maudlin's charge,[2] —   555
Hence, brain-sick fool!" — He raised his bow:—
"Now, if thou strik'st her but one blow,
I'll pitch thee from the cliff as far
As ever peasant pitch'd a bar!" — [3]

[1] two streams which flow from the Perthshire uplands into the Stirling region, and give their waters to the Forth
[2] an institution for the insane called St. Mary Magdalen. The English pronunciation is as here spelled.
[3] This used to be a favorite athletic sport in Scotland.

"Thanks, champion, thanks!" the Maniac cried, 560
And press'd her to Fitz-James's side.
"See the grey pennons [1] I prepare,
To seek my true love through the air!
I will not lend that savage groom,[2]
To break his fall, one downy plume!   565
No! — deep amid disjointed stones,
The wolves shall batten [3] on his bones,
And then shall his detested plaid,
By bush and brier in mid-air staid,
Wave forth a banner fair and free,   570
Meet signal for their revelry."—

XXIV

"Hush thee, poor maiden, and be still!" —
"O! thou look'st kindly, and I will. —
Mine eye has dried and wasted been,
But still it loves the Lincoln green;   575
And, though mine ear is all unstrung,
Still, still it loves the Lowland tongue.

"For O my sweet William was forester true,
    He stole poor Blanche's heart away!
His coat it was all of the greenwood hue,   580
    And so blithely he trill'd the Lowland lay!

"It was not that I meant to tell . . .
But thou art wise and guessest well."
Then, in a low and broken tone,
And hurried note, the song went on.   585
Still on the Clansman,[4] fearfully,
She fix'd her apprehensive eye;
Then turn'd it on the Knight,[5] and then
Her look glanced wildly o'er the glen.

[1] wings. She is preparing to fly to her murdered lover.
[2] Red Murdoch   [3] fatten   [4] Red Murdoch   [5] James Fitz-James

XXV

"The toils are pitch'd,[1] and the stakes are set,   590
  Ever sing merrily, merrily;
The bows they bend, and the knives they whet,
  Hunters live so cheerily.

"It was a stag, a stag of ten,[2]
  Bearing its branches sturdily;   595
He came stately down the glen,
  Ever sing hardily, hardily.

"It was there he met with a wounded doe,
  She was bleeding deathfully;
She warn'd him of the toils below,   600
  O so faithfully, faithfully!

"He had an eye, and he could heed,
  Ever sing warily, warily;
He had a foot, and he could speed —
  Hunters watch so narrowly."   605

XXVI

Fitz-James's mind was passion-toss'd,
When Ellen's hints and fears were lost;
But Murdoch's shout suspicion wrought,
And Blanche's song conviction brought. —
Not like a stag that spies the snare,   610
But lion of the hunt aware,
He waved at once his blade on high,
"Disclose thy treachery, or die!"
Forth at full speed the Clansman flew,
But in his race his bow he drew.   615
The shaft just grazed Fitz-James's crest,

---

[1] The Knight of Snowdoun is warned of approaching danger.
[2] "a stag having ten branches on its antlers."   Scott.

And thrilled [1] in Blanche's faded breast. —
Murdoch of Alpine! prove thy speed,
For ne'er had Alpine's son such need!
With heart of fire, and foot of wind,   620
The fierce avenger is behind!
Fate judges of the rapid strife —
The forfeit death — the prize is life!
Thy kindred ambush lies before,
Close couch'd upon the heathery moor;   625
Them couldst thou reach! — it may not be —
Thine ambush'd kin thou ne'er shalt see,
The fiery Saxon gains on thee!
— Resistless speeds the deadly thrust,
As lightning strikes the pine to dust;   630
With foot and hand Fitz-James must strain,
Ere he can win his blade again.
Bent o'er the fall'n, with falcon eye,
He grimly smiled to see him die;
Then slower wended back his way,   635
Where the poor maiden bleeding lay.

XXVII

She sate beneath a birchen-tree,
Her elbow resting on her knee;
She had withdrawn the fatal shaft,
And gazed on it, and feebly laugh'd;   640
Her wreath of broom and feathers grey,
Daggled [2] with blood, beside her lay.
The Knight to staunch the life-stream tried, —
"Stranger, it is in vain!" she cried.
"This hour of death has given me more   645
Of reason's power than years before;
For, as these ebbing veins decay,

_____
[1] pierced   [2] wet, soaked

My frenzied [1] visions fade away.
A helpless injured wretch I die,
And something tells me in thine eye,　　　　650
That thou wert mine avenger born. —
Seest thou this tress? — Oh, still I've worn
This little tress of yellow hair,
Through danger, frenzy, and despair!
It once was bright and clear as thine,　　　　655
But blood and tears have dimm'd its shine.
I will not tell thee when 'twas shred, [2]
Nor from what guiltless victim's head —
My brain would turn! — but it shall wave
Like plumage on thy helmet brave,　　　　660
Till sun and wind shall bleach the stain,
And thou wilt bring it me again. —
I waver still. — O God! more bright
Let reason beam her parting light! —
O! by thy knighthood's honour'd sign,　　　　665
And for thy life preserved by mine,
When thou shalt see a darksome man,
Who boasts him Chief of Alpine's Clan,
With tartans broad and shadowy plume
And hand of blood, and brow of gloom,　　　　670
Be thy heart bold, thy weapon strong,
And wreak [3] poor Blanche of Devan's wrong! —
They watch for thee by pass and fell . . .
Avoid the path . . . O God! . . . farewell."

XXVIII

A kindly heart had brave Fitz-James;　　　　675
Fast pour'd his eyes at pity's claims, [4]
And now, with mingled grief and ire,
He saw the murder'd maid expire.

---

[1] distracted　　　[2] cut　　　[3] avenge　　　[4] In pity was he moved to weep.

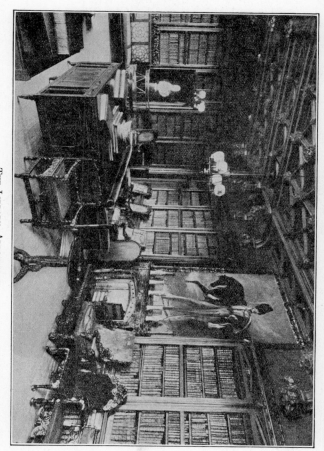

THE LIBRARY, ABBOTSFORD
Photo by Ewing Galloway.

"God, in my need, be my relief,
As I wreak this on yonder Chief!"   680
A lock from Blanche's tresses fair
He blended with her bridegroom's hair;
The mingled braid in blood he dyed,
And placed it on his bonnet-side:
"By Him whose word is truth! I swear,   685
No other favour will I wear,
Till this sad token I imbrue [1]
In the best blood of Roderick Dhu!
— But hark! what means yon faint halloo?
The chase is up, — but they shall know,   690
The stag at bay's a dangerous foe."
Barr'd from the known but guarded way,
Through copse and cliffs Fitz-James must stray,
And oft must change his desperate track,
By stream and precipice turn'd back.   695
Heartless, fatigued, and faint, at length,
From lack of food and loss of strength,
He couch'd him [2] in a thicket hoar,
And thought his toils and perils o'er: —
"Of all my rash adventures past,   700
This frantic feat must prove the last!
Who e'er so mad but might have guess'd,
That all this Highland hornet's nest
Would muster up in swarms so soon
As e'er they heard of bands [3] at Doune? —   705
Like bloodhounds now they search me out, —
Hark, to the whistle and the shout! —
If further through the wilds I go,
I only fall upon the foe:
I'll couch me here till evening grey,   710
Then darkling [4] try my dangerous way."

[1] drench   [2] lay down
[3] troops   [4] in the dark

XXIX

The shades of eve come slowly down,
The woods are wrapped in deeper brown,
The owl awakens from her dell,
The fox is heard upon the fell;   715
Enough remains of glimmering light
To guide the wanderer's steps aright,
Yet not enough from far to show
His figure to the watchful foe.
With cautious step, and ear awake,   720
He climbs the crag and threads the brake;
And not the summer solstice,[1] there,
Tempered the midnight mountain air,
But every breeze, that swept the wold,
Benumb'd his drenched limbs with cold.   725
In dread, in danger, and alone,
Famish'd and chill'd, through ways unknown,
Tangled and steep, he journey'd on;
Till, as a rock's huge point he turn'd,
A watch-fire close before him burn'd.   730

XXX

Beside its embers red and clear,
Bask'd, in his plaid, a mountaineer;
And up he sprung with sword in hand, —
"Thy name and purpose! Saxon, stand!"
"A stranger."   "What dost thou require?" —   735
"Rest and a guide, and food and fire.
My life's beset, my path is lost,
The gale has chill'd my limbs with frost." —
"Art thou a friend to Roderick?" "No."
"Thou darest not call thyself a foe?"   740
"I dare! to him and all the band

---

[1] the longest day of the year, when the heat is supposed to be the greatest

He brings to aid his murderous hand." —
"Bold words! — but, though the beast of game
The privilege of chase may claim,
Though space and law the stag we lend,   745
Ere hound we slip,[1] or bow we bend,
Who ever reck'd,[2] where, how, or when,
The prowling fox was trapp'd or slain?
Thus treacherous scouts, — yet sure they lie,
Who say thou camest a secret spy!" —   750
"They do, by heaven! — Come Roderick Dhu,
And of his clan the boldest two,
And let me but till morning rest,
I write the falsehood on their crest."
"If by the blaze I mark aright,   755
Thou bear'st the belt and spur of Knight."
"Then by these tokens may'st thou know
Each proud oppressor's mortal foe." —
"Enough, enough; sit down and share
A soldier's couch, a soldier's fare."   760

XXXI

He gave him of his Highland cheer,
The harden'd flesh of mountain deer;
Dry fuel on the fire he laid,
And bade the Saxon share his plaid.
He tended him like welcome guest,   765
Then thus his further speech address'd: —
"Stranger, I am to Roderick Dhu
A clansman born, a kinsman true;
Each word against his honour spoke,
Demands of me avenging stroke;   770
Yet more, — upon thy fate, 'tis said,
A mighty augury[3] is laid.
It rests with me to wind my horn, —

---

[1] let loose   [2] cared   [3] the Taghairm

Thou art with numbers overborne;
It rests with me, here, brand to brand, 775
Worn as thou art, to bid thee stand:
But, not for clan, nor kindred's cause,
Will I depart from honour's laws;
To assail a wearied man were shame,
And stranger is a holy name; 780
Guidance and rest, and food and fire,
In vain he never must require.
Then rest thee here till dawn of day;
Myself will guide thee on the way,
O'er stock and stone, through watch and ward, 785
Till past Clan-Alpine's outmost guard,
As far as Coilantogle's ford;
From thence thy warrant is thy sword."
"I take thy courtesy, by heaven,
As freely as 'tis nobly given!" 790
"Well, rest thee; for the bittern's [1] cry
Sings us the lake's wild lullaby."
With that he shook the gather'd heath,
And spread his plaid upon the wreath;
And the brave foemen, side by side, 795
Lay peaceful down like brothers tried,
And slept until the dawning beam
Purpled the mountain and the stream.

CANTO FIFTH

THE COMBAT

I

FAIR as the earliest beam of eastern light,
    When first, by the bewilder'd pilgrim spied,
It smiles upon the dreary brow of night,

---

[1] a bird having a shrill, mournful cry

And silvers o'er the torrent's foaming tide,
And lights the fearful path on mountain side; —   5
    Fair as that beam, although the fairest far,
Giving to horror grace, to danger pride,
    Shine martial Faith, and Courtesy's bright star,
Through all the wreckful storms that cloud the brow
        of War.

II

That early beam, so fair and sheen,[1]   10
Was twinkling through the hazel screen,
When, rousing at its glimmer red,
The warriors left their lowly bed,
Look'd out upon the dappled sky,
Mutter'd their soldier matins by,[2]   15
And then awaked their fire, to steal,[3]
As short and rude, their soldier meal.
That o'er, the Gael [4] around him threw
His graceful plaid of varied hue,
And, true to promise, led the way,   20
By thicket green and mountain grey.
A wildering [5] path! — they winded now
Along the precipice's brow,
Commanding the rich scenes beneath,
The windings of the Forth and Teith,   25
And all the vales between that lie,
Till Stirling's turrets melt in sky;
Then, sunk in copse, their farthest glance
Gain'd not the length of horseman's lance.
'Twas oft so steep, the foot was fain [6]   30
Assistance from the hand to gain;
So tangled oft, that, bursting through,
Each hawthorn shed her showers of dew, —

---

[1] bright   [2] muttered their morning prayers hurriedly
[3] to eat their meal hastily   [4] highlander. The Lowlander is called "Saxon."
[5] bewildering   [6] glad

That diamond dew, so pure and clear,
It rivals all but Beauty's tear!   35

III

At length they came where, stern and steep,
The hill sinks down upon the deep.
Here Vennachar in silver flows,
There, ridge on ridge, Ben Ledi rose;
Ever the hollow path twined on,   40
Beneath steep bank and threatening stone;
An hundred men might hold the post
With hardihood against a host.
The rugged mountain's scanty cloak
Was dwarfish shrubs of birch and oak,   45
With shingles ¹ bare, and cliffs between,
And patches bright of bracken green,
And heather black, that waved so high,
It held the copse in rivalry.
But where the lake slept deep and still,   50
Dank osiers ² fringed the swamp and hill;
And oft both path and hill were torn,
Where wintry torrents down had borne,
And heap'd upon the cumber'd ³ land
Its wreck of gravel, rocks, and sand.   55
So toilsome was the road to trace,
The guide, abating of his pace,
Led slowly through the pass's jaws,
And ask'd Fitz-James, by what strange cause
He sought these wilds? traversed by few,   60
Without a pass from Roderick Dhu.

IV

"Brave Gael, my pass, in danger tried,
Hangs in my belt, and by my side;

¹ gravel, pebbles   ² damp willows   ³ encumbered

Yet, sooth to tell," the Saxon said,
"I dreamt not now to claim its aid,   65
When here, but three days since, I came,
Bewilder'd in pursuit of game,
All seem'd as peaceful and as still,
As the mist slumbering on yon hill;
Thy dangerous Chief was then afar,   70
Nor soon expected back from war.
Thus said, at least, my mountain-guide,
Though deep perchance the villain lied." —
"Yet why a second venture try?" —
"A warrior thou, and ask me why! —   75
Moves our free course by such fix'd cause,
As gives the poor mechanic laws?
Enough, I sought to drive away
The lazy hours of peaceful day;
Slight cause will then suffice to guide   80
A Knight's free footsteps far and wide, —
A falcon flown, a greyhound stray'd,
The merry glance of mountain maid:
Or, if a path be dangerous known,
The danger's self is lure alone." —   85

V

"Thy secret keep, I urge thee not; —
Yet, ere again ye sought this spot,
Say, heard ye nought of Lowland war,
Against Clan-Alpine, raised by Mar?"
— "No, by my word; — of bands prepared   90
To guard King James's sports I heard;
Nor doubt I aught, but, when they hear
This muster of the mountaineer,
Their pennons will abroad be flung,
Which else in Doune had peaceful hung." —   95

"Free be they flung! — for we were loth
Their silken folds should feast the moth.
Free be they flung! — as free shall wave
Clan-Alpine's pine in banner brave.
But, Stranger, peaceful since you came,   100
Bewilder'd in the mountain game,
Whence the bold boast by which you show
Vich-Alpine's vow'd and mortal foe?" —
"Warrior, but yester-morn, I knew
Nought of thy Chieftain, Roderick Dhu,   105
Save as an outlaw'd desperate man,
The chief of a rebellious clan,
Who, in the Regent's [1] court and sight,
With ruffian dagger stabb'd a knight:
Yet this alone might from his part   110
Sever each true and loyal heart."

VI

Wrothful at such arraignment foul,
Dark lower'd the clansman's sable scowl.
A space he paused, then sternly said,
"And heard'st thou why he drew his blade?   115
Heard'st thou that shameful word and blow
Brought Roderick's vengeance on his foe?
What reck'd the Chieftain if he stood
On Highland heath, or Holy-Rood?
He rights such wrong where it is given,   120
If it were in the court of heaven." —
"Still was it outrage; — yet, 'tis true,
Not then claim'd sovereignty his due;
While Albany, with feeble hand,
Held borrow'd truncheon [2] of command,   125
The young King, mew'd [3] in Stirling tower,

[1] John Stuart, Duke of Albany, was regent or ruler during the minority of
James V.   [2] staff   [3] imprisoned

Was stranger to respect and power.
But then, thy Chieftain's robber life! —
Winning mean prey by causeless strife,
Wrenching from ruin'd Lowland swain   130
His herds and harvest reared in vain. —
Methinks a soul, like thine, should scorn
The spoils from such foul foray borne."

VII

The Gael beheld him grim the while,
And answer'd with disdainful smile, —   135
"Saxon, from yonder mountain high,
I mark'd thee send delighted eye,
Far to the south and east, where lay,
Extended in succession gay,
Deep waving fields and pastures green,   140
With gentle slopes and groves between: —
These fertile plains, that soften'd vale,
Were once the birthright of the Gael;
The stranger came with iron hand,
And from our fathers reft [1] the land.   145
Where dwell we now! See, rudely swell
Crag over crag, and fell o'er fell.
Ask we this savage hill we tread,
For fatten'd steer or household bread;
Ask we for flocks these shingles dry,   150
And well the mountain might reply, —
'To you, as to your sires of yore,
Belong the target and claymore!
I give you shelter in my breast,
Your own good blades must win the rest.'   155
Pent in this fortress of the North,
Think'st thou we will not sally forth,
To spoil the spoiler as we may,

[1] snatched

And from the robber rend the prey?
Ay, by my soul! — While on yon plain   160
The Saxon rears one shock of grain;
While, of ten thousand herds, there strays
But one along yon river's maze, —
The Gael, of plain and river heir,
Shall, with strong hand, redeem his share.   165
Where live the mountain Chiefs who hold
That plundering Lowland field and fold
Is aught but retribution true?
Seek other cause 'gainst Roderick Dhu." — [1]

VIII

Answer'd Fitz-James, — "And, if I sought,   170
Think'st thou no other could be brought?
What deem ye of my path waylaid?
My life given o'er to ambuscade?" —
"As of a meed [2] to rashness due:
Hadst thou sent warning fair and true, —   175
I seek my hound, or falcon stray'd,
I seek, good faith, a Highland maid, —
Free hadst thou been to come and go;
But secret path marks secret foe.
Nor yet, for this, even as a spy,   180
Hadst thou, unheard, been doom'd to die,
Save to fulfill an augury." [3]
"Well, let it pass; nor will I now

[1] "So far, indeed, was a *Creagh*, or foray, from being held disgraceful, that a young chief was always expected to show his talents for command, so soon as he assumed it, by leading his clan on a successful enterprise of this nature, either against a neighboring sept, for which constant feuds usually furnished an apology, or against the Saxons, or Lowlanders, for which no apology was necessary. The Gael, great traditional historians, never forgot that the Lowlands had, at some remote period, been the property of their Celtic forefathers, which furnished an ample vindication of all the ravages that they could make on the unfortunate districts which lay within their reach."   Scott.

[2] reward

[3] the Taghairm

Fresh cause of enmity avow,
To chafe thy mood and cloud thy brow.   185
Enough, I am by promise tied
To match me with this man of pride:
Twice have I sought Clan-Alpine's glen
In peace; but when I come agen,
I come with banner, brand, and bow,   190
As leader seeks his mortal foe.
For love-lorn swain, in lady's bower,
Ne'er panted for the appointed hour,
As I, until before me stand
This rebel Chieftain and his band!"   195

IX

"Have, then, thy wish!" — He whistled shrill,
And he was answer'd from the hill;
Wild as the scream of the curlew,[1]
From crag to crag the signal flew.
Instant, through copse and heath, arose   200
Bonnets and spears and bended bows;
On right, on left, above, below,
Sprung up at once the lurking foe;
From shingles grey their lances start,
The bracken bush sends forth the dart,   205
The rushes and the willow-wand
Are bristling into axe and brand,
And every tuft of broom gives life
To plaided warrior arm'd for strife.
That whistle garrison'd the glen [2]   210
At once with full five hundred men,
As if the yawning hill to heaven
A subterranean host had given.

---

[1] a shore bird. In summer it is found among the mountains; in winter it fre-
quents the seashore.
[2] manned the glen

Watching their leader's beck and will,
All silent there they stood, and still.   215
Like the loose crags whose threatening mass
Lay tottering o'er the hollow pass,
As if an infant's touch could urge
Their headlong passage down the verge,[1]
With step and weapon forward flung,   220
Upon the mountain-side they hung.
The Mountaineer cast glance of pride
Along Ben Ledi's living side,
Then fix'd his eye and sable brow
Full on Fitz-James — "How say'st thou now?   225
These are Clan-Alpine's warriors true;
And, Saxon, — I am Roderick Dhu!"

X

Fitz-James was brave: — Though to his heart
The life-blood thrill'd with sudden start,
He mann'd himself with dauntless air,   230
Return'd the Chief his haughty stare,
His back against a rock he bore,
And firmly placed his foot before: —
"Come one, come all! this rock shall fly
From its firm base as soon as I."   235
Sir Roderick mark'd — and in his eyes
Respect was mingled with surprise,
And the stern joy which warriors feel
In foemen worthy of their steel.
Short space he stood — then waved his hand: 240
Down sunk the disappearing band;
Each warrior vanish'd where he stood,
In broom or bracken, heath or wood;
Sunk brand and spear and bended bow,
In osiers pale and copses low;   245

---

[1] precipice

It seemed as if their mother Earth
Had swallow'd up her warlike birth.
The wind's last breath had toss'd in air,
Pennon, and plaid, and plumage fair, —
The next but swept a lone hill-side,   250
Where heath and fern were waving wide:
The sun's last glance was glinted back,
From spear and glaive, from targe and jack,[1] —
The next, all unreflected, shone
On bracken green, and cold grey stone.   255

XI

Fitz-James look'd round — yet scarce believed
The witness that his sight received;
Such apparition well might seem
Delusion of a dreadful dream.
Sir Roderick in suspense he eyed,   260
And to his look the Chief replied,
"Fear nought — nay, that I need not say —
But — doubt not aught from mine array.
Thou art my guest; — I pledged my word
As far as Coilantogle ford: 265
Nor would I call a clansman's brand
For aid against one valiant hand,
Though on our strife lay every vale
Rent by the Saxon from the Gael.
So move we on; — I only meant   270
To show the reed on which you leant,
Deeming this path you might pursue
Without a pass from Roderick Dhu."[2]
They moved: — I said Fitz-James was brave,

[1] from shield and coat of armor. The peasant's armor consisted of a leathern jacket.

[2] Like other passages in this poem this incident is based on fact. "The Highlanders, with the inconsistency of most nations in the same state, were alternately capable of great exertions of generosity, and of cruel revenge and perfidy." Scott.

As ever knight that belted glaive;   275
Yet dare not say, that now his blood
Kept on its wont and temper'd flood,
As, following Roderick's stride, he drew
That seeming lonesome pathway through,
Which yet, by fearful proof, was rife   280
With lances, that, to take his life,
Waited but signal from a guide,
So late dishonour'd and defied.
Ever, by stealth, his eye sought round
The vanish'd guardians of the ground,   285
And still, from copse and heather deep,
Fancy saw spear and broadsword peep,
And in the plover's [1] shrilly strain,
The signal whistle heard again.
Nor breathed he free till far behind   290
The pass was left; for then they wind
Along a wide and level green,
Where neither tree nor tuft was seen,
Nor rush nor bush of broom was near,
To hide a bonnet or a spear.   295

XII

The Chief in silence strode before,
And reached that torrent's sounding shore,
Which, daughter of three mighty lakes,[2]
From Vennachar in silver breaks,
Sweeps through the plain, and ceaseless mines   300
On Bochastle the mouldering lines,
Where Rome, the Empress of the world,
Of yore her eagle wings unfurl'd.[3]
And here his course the Chieftain staid,

[1] a bird frequenting the seashore and banks of rivers
[2] Katrine, Achray, and Vennachar
[3] The eagle was the principal standard of the Roman army.

Threw down his target and his plaid,   305
And to the Lowland warrior said —
"Bold Saxon! to his promise just,
Vich-Alpine has discharged his trust.
This murderous Chief, this ruthless man,
This head of a rebellious clan,   310
Hath led thee safe, through watch and ward,
Far past Clan-Alpine's outmost guard.
Now, man to man, and steel to steel,
A Chieftain's vengeance thou shalt feel.
See, here, all vantageless I stand,   315
Arm'd, like thyself, with single brand:
For this is Coilantogle ford,
And thou must keep thee with thy sword."

XIII

The Saxon paused: — "I ne'er delay'd,
When foeman bade me draw my blade;   320
Nay more, brave Chief, I vow'd thy death:
Yet sure thy fair and generous faith,
And my deep debt for life preserved,
A better meed have well deserved:
Can nought but blood our feud atone?   325
Are there no means?" — "No, Stranger, none!
And hear, — to fire thy flagging zeal, —
The Saxon cause rests on thy steel;
For thus spoke Fate, by prophet bred
Between the living and the dead;   330
'Who spills the foremost foeman's life,
His party conquers in the strife.' " [1]
"Then, by my word," the Saxon said,
"The riddle is already read.
Seek yonder brake beneath the cliff, —   335
There lies Red Murdoch, stark and stiff.

[1] the prophecy of Brian. Read Stanza VI, Canto IV.

Thus Fate has solved her prophecy,[1]
Then yield to Fate, and not to me.
To James, at Stirling, let us go,
When, if thou wilt be still his foe,   340
Or if the King shall not agree
To grant thee grace and favour free,[2]
I plight mine honour, oath, and word,
That, to thy native strengths [3] restored,
With each advantage shalt thou stand,   345
That aids thee now to guard thy land."

XIV

Dark lightning flash'd from Roderick's eye —
"Soars thy presumption, then, so high,
Because a wretched kern ye slew,
Homage to name to Roderick Dhu?   350
He yields not, he, to man nor Fate!
Thou add'st but fuel to my hate. —
My clansman's blood demands revenge.
Not yet prepared? — By heaven, I change
My thought, and hold thy valour light   355
As that of some vain carpet knight,[4]
Who ill deserved my courteous care,
And whose best boast is but to wear
A braid of his fair lady's hair." —
"I thank thee, Roderick, for the word!   360
It nerves my heart, it steels my sword;
For I have sworn this braid to stain
In the best blood that warms thy vein.
Now, truce, farewell! and, ruth,[5] begone! —
Yet think not that by thee alone,   365
Proud Chief! can courtesy be shown;

[1] Roderick will be defeated.   [2] complete   [3] strongholds
[4] one who wins favor in the drawing-room of a castle and not on the battlefields
[5] pity, an obsolete word; however, we do have *ruthless*.

Though not from copse, or heath, or cairn,
Start at my whistle clansmen stern,
Of this small horn one feeble blast
Would fearful odds against thee cast.   370
But fear not — doubt not — which thou wilt —
We try this quarrel hilt to hilt." —
Then each at once his falchion drew,
Each on the ground his scabbard threw,
Each look'd to sun, and stream, and plain,   375
As what they ne'er might see again;
Then foot, and point, and eye opposed,
In dubious strife they darkly closed.

XV

Ill fared it then with Roderick Dhu,
That on the field his targe he threw,[1]   380
Whose brazen studs and tough bull-hide
Had death so often dash'd aside;
For, train'd abroad [2] his arms to wield,
Fitz-James's blade was sword and shield.
He practised every pass and ward,   385
To thrust, to strike, to feint, to guard;
While less expert, though stronger far,
The Gael maintain'd unequal war.
Three times in closing strife they stood,
And thrice the Saxon blade drank blood;   390
No stinted draught, no scanty tide,
The gushing flood the tartans dyed.
Fierce Roderick felt the fatal drain,
And shower'd his blows like wintry rain;
And, as firm rock, or castle-roof,   395

[1] "A round target of light wood, covered with strong leather and studded with brass or iron, was a necessary part of a Highlander's equipment. In charging regular troops they received the thrust of the bayonet in this buckler, twisted it aside, and used the broadsword against the encumbered soldier." Scott.

[2] in France, where the best swordsmen are still found

Against the winter shower is proof,
The foe, invulnerable still,
Foil'd his wild rage by steady skill;
Till, at advantage ta'en, his brand
Forced Roderick's weapon from his hand,   400
And backward borne upon the lea,
Brought the proud Chieftain to his knee.

XVI

"Now, yield thee, or by Him who made
The world, thy heart's blood dyes my blade!"—
"Thy threats, thy mercy, I defy!   405
Let recreant [1] yield, who fears to die."
— Like adder darting from his coil,
Like wolf that dashes through the toil,
Like mountain-cat who guards her young,
Full at Fitz-James's throat he sprung;   410
Received, but reck'd not of a wound,
And lock'd his arms his foeman round. —
Now, gallant Saxon, hold thine own!
No maiden's hand is round thee thrown!
That desperate grasp thy frame might feel,   415
Through bars of brass and triple steel! —
They tug, they strain! down, down they go,
The Gael above, Fitz-James below.
The Chieftain's gripe his throat compress'd
His knee was planted in his breast;   420
His clotted locks he backward threw,
Across his brow his hand he drew,
From blood and mist to clear his sight,
Then gleam'd aloft his dagger bright! —
— But hate. and fury ill supplied   425
The stream of life's exhausted tide,

[1] coward

And all too late the advantage came,
To turn the odds of deadly game;
For, while the dagger gleam'd on high,
Reel'd soul and sense, reel'd brain and eye.   430
Down came the blow! but in the heath
The erring blade found bloodless sheath.
The struggling foe may now unclasp
The fainting Chief's relaxing grasp;
Unwounded from the dreadful close,[1]   435
But breathless all, Fitz-James arose.

XVII

He falter'd thanks to Heaven for life,
Redeem'd, unhoped, from desperate strife;
Next on his foe his look he cast,
Whose every gasp appear'd his last;   440
In Roderick's gore he dipped the braid, —
"Poor Blanche! thy wrongs are dearly paid:
Yet with thy foe must die, or live,
The praise that faith and valour give."
With that he blew a bugle-note,   445
Undid the collar from his throat,
Unbonneted, and by the wave
Sate down his brow and hands to lave.
Then faint afar are heard the feet
Of rushing steeds in gallop fleet;   450
The sounds increase, and now are seen
Four mounted squires [2] in Lincoln green;
Two who bear lance, and two who lead,
By loosen'd rein, a saddled steed;
Each onward held his headlong course,   455
And by Fitz-James rein'd up his horse, —
With wonder view'd the bloody spot —
— "Exclaim not, gallants! [3] question not. —

[1] grapple   [2] a knight's attendants   [3] fearless people

You, Herbert and Luffness, alight,
And bind the wounds of yonder knight;   460
Let the grey palfrey ¹ bear his weight,
We destined for a fairer freight,²
And bring him on to Stirling straight;
I will before ³ at better speed,
To seek fresh horse and fitting weed.⁴   465
The sun rides high; — I must be boune,⁵
To see the archer-game at noon;
But lightly Bayard clears the lea. —
De Vaux and Herries, follow me."

XVIII

"Stand, Bayard, stand!" — the steed obey'd,   470
With arching neck and bended head,
And glancing eye and quivering ear
As if he loved his lord to hear.
No foot Fitz-James in stirrup staid,
No grasp upon the saddle laid,   475
But wreath'd his left hand in the mane
And lightly bounded from the plain,
Turn'd on the horse his armed heel,
And stirr'd his courage with the steel.
Bounded the fiery steed in air,   480
The rider sate erect and fair,
Then like a bolt from steel crossbow
Forth launch'd, along the plain they go.
They dash'd that rapid torrent through,
And up Carhonie's hill ⁶ they flew;   485
Still at the gallop prick'd ⁷ the Knight,
His merry-men follow'd as they might.
Along thy banks, swift Teith! they ride,

¹ a small saddle horse used by ladies
² Ellen   ³ proceed before   ⁴ clothes   ⁵ ready
⁶ a hill about a mile from the lower end of Loch Vennachar
⁷ spurred or rode

And in the race they mock thy tide;
Torry and Lendrick now are past,   490
And Deanstown lies behind them cast;
They rise, the banner'd towers of Doune.[1]
They sink in distant woodland soon;
Blair-Drummond sees the hoofs strike fire,
They sweep like breeze through Ochtertyre;   495
They mark just glance and disappear
The lofty brow of ancient Kier;
They bathe their courser's sweltering sides,
Dark Forth! amid thy sluggish tides,
And on the opposing shore take ground,   500
With plash, with scramble, and with bound.
Right-hand they leave thy cliffs, Craig-Forth!
And soon the bulwark of the North,
Grey Stirling, with her towers and town,
Upon their fleet career look'd down.   505

XIX

As up the flinty path they strain'd
Sudden his steed the leader rein'd;
A signal to his squire he flung,
Who instant to his stirrup sprung: —
"Seest thou, De Vaux, yon woodsman grey,   510
Who town-ward holds the rocky way,
Of stature tall and poor array?
Mark'st thou the firm, yet active stride,
With which he scales the mountain-side?
Know'st thou from whence he comes, or whom?"515
"No, by my word; — a burly groom
He seems, who in the field or chase
A baron's train would nobly grace." —
"Out, out, De Vaux! can fear supply,
And jealousy, no sharper eye?   520

[1] the ruins of Doune Castle

Afar, ere to the hill he drew,
That stately form and step I knew;
Like form in Scotland is not seen,
Treads not such step on Scottish green.
'Tis James of Douglas, by Saint Serle! [1]   525
The uncle of the banish'd Earl.
Away, away, to court, to show
The near approach of dreaded foe:
The King must stand upon his guard;
Douglas and he must meet prepared."   530
Then right-hand wheel'd their steeds, and straight
They won the castle's postern [2] gate.

XX

The Douglas, who had bent his way
From Cambus-Kenneth's abbey grey,
Now, as he climb'd the rocky shelf,   535
Held sad communion with himself: —
"Yes! all is true my fears could frame;
A prisoner lies the noble Graeme,
And fiery Roderick soon will feel
The vengeance of the royal steel.   540
I, only I, can ward their fate, —
God grant the ransom come not late!
The Abbess hath her promise given,
My child shall be the bride of heaven; [3] —
— Be pardon'd one repining tear!   545
For He, who gave her, knows how dear,
How excellent! — but that is by, [4]
And now my business is — to die.
— Ye towers! within whose circuit dread
A Douglas [5] by his sovereign bled;   550

[1] Scott invented this name to rhyme with *Earl*.   [2] rear   [3] nun   [4] past
[5] "The fate of William, eighth Earl of Douglas, whom James II stabbed in Stirling Castle with his own hand, and while under his royal safe conduct, is familiar to all who read Scottish history." Scott.

And thou, O sad and fatal mound! [1]
That oft has heard the death-axe sound,
As on the noblest of the land
Fell the stern headsman's bloody hand, —
The dungeon, block, and nameless tomb   555
Prepare — for Douglas seeks his doom!
— But hark! what blithe and jolly peal
Makes the Franciscan [2] steeple reel?
And see! upon the crowded street,
In motley groups what masquers meet!   560
Banner and pageant, pipe and drum,
And merry morrice-dancers [3] come.
I guess, by all this quaint array,
The burghers hold their sports to-day. [4]
James will be there; he loves such show,   565
Where the good yeomen bends his bow,
And the tough wrestler foils his foe,
As well as where, in proud career,
The high-born tilter shivers spear.
I'll follow to the Castle-park,   570
And play my prize; — King James shall mark,
If age has tamed these sinews stark,
Whose force so oft, in happier days,
His boyish wonder loved to praise."

XXI

The Castle gates were open flung,   575
The quivering drawbridge rock'd and rung,
And echo'd loud the flinty street
Beneath the coursers' clattering feet,

[1] "an eminence on the north-east of the Stirling Castle where state criminals were executed. Stirling was often polluted with noble blood." Scott.

[2] Franciscan. A Roman Catholic order founded by St. Francis on the principle of poverty. The steeple is on Greyfriars' Church.

[3] The morrice-dance was a Spanish dance popular in England at the May-day games.

[4] a festival usually held annually with games and a play

As slowly down the steep descent
Fair Scotland's King and nobles went,   580
While all along the crowded way
Was jubilee and loud huzza.
And ever James was bending low,
To his white jennet's [1] saddle-bow,
Doffing his cap to city dame,   585
Who smiled and blush'd for pride and shame.
And well the simperer [2] might be vain, —
He chose the fairest of the train.
Gravely he greets each city sire,
Commends each pageant's quaint attire,   590
Gives to the dancers thanks aloud,
And smiles and nods upon the crowd,
Who rend the heavens with their acclaims,
"Long live the Commons' King,[3] King James!"
Behind the King throng'd peer and knight,   595
And noble dame and damsel bright,
Whose fiery steeds ill brook'd the stay
Of the steep street and crowded way.
— But in the train you might discern
Dark lowering brow and visage stern;   600
There nobles mourn'd their pride restrain'd,
And the mean burgher's joys disdain'd;
And chiefs, who, hostage [4] for their clan,
Were each from home a banish'd man,
There thought upon their own grey tower,   605
Their waving woods, their feudal power,[5]
And deem'd themselves a shameful part
Of pageant which they cursed in heart.

---

[1] small Spanish horse
[2] one who smiles coyly
[3] He was so called because he favored the common people instead of the nobility.
[4] a person held as security until the provisions of an agreement are satisfactorily carried out
[5] the power to command the services of tenants during a war

XXII

Now, in the Castle-park, drew out
Their chequer'd bands [1] the joyous rout.[2]   610
There morricers, with bell at heel,
And blade in hand, their mazes wheel;
But chief, beside the butts,[3] there stand
Bold Robin Hood [4] and all his band, —
Friar Tuck [5] with quarterstaff and cowl,[6]   615
Old Scathelocke with his surly scowl,
Maid Marion, fair as ivory bone,
Scarlet, and Mutch, and Little John;
Their bugles challenge all that will,
In archery to prove their skill.   620
The Douglas bent a bow of might, —
His first shaft centred in the white,
And when in turn he shot again,
His second split the first in twain.
From the King's hand must Douglas take   625
A silver dart,[7] the archer's stake;
Fondly he watch'd, with watery eye,
Some answering glance of sympathy,—
No kind emotion made reply!
Indifferent as to archer wight,[8]   630
The monarch gave the arrow bright.

XXIII

Now, clear the ring! for, hand to hand,
The manly wrestlers take their stand.
Two o'er the rest superior rose,
And proud demanded mightier foes,   635

---

[1] various squads in gay costumes   [2] noisy throng   [3] targets
[4] Robin Hood was a favorite impersonation.
[5] These were Robin Hood's companions. Read about them in Scott's *Ivanhoe.*
[6] the hood of a monk
[7] the usual prize in archery
[8] common archer

Nor call'd in vain; for Douglas came.
— For life is Hugh of Larbert [1] lame;
Scarce better John of Alloa's fare,
Whom senseless home his comrades bear.
Prize of the wrestling match, the King   640
To Douglas gave a golden ring,
While coldly glanced his eye of blue,
As frozen drop of wintry dew.
Douglas would speak, but in his breast
His struggling soul his words suppress'd;   645
Indignant then he turn'd him where
Their arms the brawny yeomen bare,
To hurl the massive bar [2] in air.
When each his utmost strength had shown,
The Douglas rent an earth-fast stone   650
From its deep bed, then heav'd it high,
And sent the fragment through the sky,
A rood beyond the farthest mark; —
And still in Stirling's royal park,
The grey-hair'd sires, who know the past,   655
To strangers point the Douglas-cast,
And moralize on the decay
Of Scottish strength in modern day.

XXIV

The vale with loud applauses rang,
The Ladies' Rock [3] sent back the clang.   660
The King, with look unmoved, bestow'd
A purse well-fill'd with pieces broad.
Indignant smiled the Douglas proud,
And threw the gold among the crowd,

[1] Hugh of the town of Larbert was seriously injured.
[2] This corresponds to our *putting the shot*.
[3] a hill between Greyfriars' Church and Stirling Castle where spectators, especially the ladies, viewed the various athletic sports

Who now, with anxious wonder, scan,   665
And sharper glance, the dark grey man;
Till whispers rose among the throng,
That heart so free, and hand so strong,
Must to the Douglas blood belong,
The old men mark'd and shook the head,   670
To see his hair with silver spread,
And wink'd aside, and told each son,
Of feats upon the English done,
Ere Douglas of the stalwart hand
Was exiled from his native land.   675
The women praised his stately form,
Though wreck'd by many a winter's storm;
The youth with awe and wonder saw
His strength surpassing Nature's law.
Thus judged, as is their wont, the crowd,   680
Till murmur rose to clamours loud.
But not a glance from that proud ring
Of peers who circled round the King,
With Douglas held communion kind,
Or call'd the banish'd man to mind;   685
No, not from those who, at the chase,
Once held his side the honour'd place,
Begirt his board,[1] and, in the field,
Found safety underneath his shield;
For he, whom royal eyes disown,   690
When was his form to courtiers known!

XXV

The Monarch saw the gambols flag,[2]
And bade let loose a gallant stag,
Whose pride, the holiday to crown,
Two favourite greyhounds should pull down,   695

---

[1] surrounded his table
[2] witnessed their loss of interest in the contest

STIRLING CASTLE

On the meadow in the foreground the knights held their tournaments and the burghers their games. Photo by Ewing Galloway.

That venison free, and Bordeaux wine,
Might serve the archery to dine.
But Lufra, — whom from Douglas' side
Nor bribe nor threat could e'er divide,[1]
The fleetest hound in all the North, —   700
Brave Lufra saw, and darted forth.
She left the royal hounds mid-way,
And dashing on the antler'd prey,
Sunk her sharp muzzle in his flank,
And deep the flowing life-blood drank.   705
The King's stout huntsman saw the sport
By strange intruder broken short,
Came up, and with his leash [2] unbound,
In anger struck the noble hound.[3]
— The Douglas had endured, that morn,   710
The King's cold look, the nobles' scorn,
And last, and worst to spirit proud,
Had borne the pity of the crowd;
But Lufra had been fondly bred,
To share his board, to watch his bed,   715
And oft would Ellen, Lufra's neck
In maiden glee with garlands deck;
They were such playmates, that with name
Of Lufra, Ellen's image came.
His stifled wrath is brimming high,   720
In darken'd brow and flashing eye;
As waves before the bark divide,
The crowd gave way before his stride;
Needs but a buffet [4] and no more,
The groom lies senseless in his gore,   725
Such blow no other hand could deal,
Though gauntleted in glove of steel.

---

[1] separate
[2] a whip or long leathern cord
[3] Remember Scott's keen interest in dogs.
[4] blow, cuff

XXVI

Then clamour'd loud the royal train,
And brandish'd swords and staves amain,
But stern the Baron's warning — "Back!   730
Back, on[1] your lives, ye menial pack![2]
Beware the Douglas. — Yes! behold,
King James! the Douglas, doom'd of old,[3]
And vainly sought for near and far,
A victim to atone the war,   735
A willing victim, now attends,
Nor craves thy grace but for his friends." —
"Thus is my clemency repaid?
Presumptuous Lord!" the Monarch said;
"Of thy mis-proud[4] ambitious clan,   740
Thou, James of Bothwell,[5] wert the man,
The only man, in whom a foe
My woman-mercy would not know:
But shall a Monarch's presence brook[6]
Injurious blow, and haughty look? —   745
What ho! the Captain of our Guard!
Give the offender fitting ward.[7]
Break off the sports!" — for tumult rose,
And yeomen 'gan to bend their bows, —
"Break off the sports!" he said, and frown'd,   750
"And bid our horsemen clear the ground."

XXVII

Then uproar wild and misarray[8]
Marr'd the fair form of festal day.
The horsemen prick'd among the crowd,
Repell'd by threats and insult loud;   755

[1] as you value	[2] pack of slaves
[3] formerly placed under the ban	[4] wrongly proud
[5] an enemy of the king	[6] hinder
[7] ward off, guard	[8] confusion

To earth are borne the old and weak,
The timorous fly, the women shriek;
With flint, with shaft, with staff, with bar,
The hardier urge tumultuous war.
At once round Douglas darkly sweep   760
The royal spears in circle deep,
And slowly scale the pathway steep;
While on the rear in thunder pour
The rabble with disorder'd roar.
With grief the noble Douglas saw   765
The Commons rise against the law,
And to the leading soldier said, —
"Sir John of Hyndford! 'twas my blade,
That knighthood [1] on thy shoulder laid;
For that good deed, permit me then   770
A word with these misguided men.

                    XXVIII

"Hear, gentle friends! ere yet for me,
Ye break the bands of fealty.[2]
My life, my honour, and my cause,
I tender free to Scotland's laws.   775
Are these so weak as must require
The aid of your misguided ire?
Or, if I suffer causeless [3] wrong,
Is then my selfish rage so strong,
My sense of public weal so low,   780
That, for mean vengeance on a foe,
Those cords of love I should unbind,
Which knit my country and my kind?
Oh, no! Believe, in yonder tower
It will not soothe my captive hour,   785

---

[1] This degree was conferred upon the candidate by striking him with the flat
part of a sword.
[2] loyalty   [3] without cause

THE GATE, STIRLING CASTLE

A moat, surmounted by a drawbridge, once protected this entrance. The narrow slits in the towers are *embrasures*, where bowmen could once let fly their arrows with slight danger to themselves. From the battlements above soldiers could drop stones on attacking forces and, in later times, could shoot cannon balls at them. Photo by Ewing Galloway.

To know those spears our foes should dread,
For me in kindred gore are red;
To know, in fruitless brawl begun,
For me, that mother wails her son;
For me, that widow's mate expires;　　　　　790
For me, that orphans weep their sires;
That patriots mourn insulted laws,
And curse the Douglas for the cause.
Oh, let your patience ward such ill,
And keep your right to love me still!"　　　　795

XXIX

The crowd's wild fury sunk again
In tears, as tempests melt in rain.
With lifted hands and eyes, they pray'd
For blessings on his generous head,
Who for his country felt alone,　　　　　800
And prized her blood beyond his own.
Old men, upon the verge of life,
Bless'd him who stay'd the civil strife;
And mothers held their babes on high,
The self-devoted Chief to spy,　　　　　805
Triumphant over wrongs and ire,
To whom the prattlers owed a sire:
Even the rough soldier's heart was moved;
As if behind some bier beloved,
With trailing arms [1] and drooping head,　　　810
The Douglas up the hill he led,
And at the castle's battled [2] verge, [3]
With sighs resign'd his honour'd charge.

---

[1] as at a military funeral

[2] Around the top of a castle was a wall with openings through which the soldiers saw the movement of troops and fired at them. These walls, called "battlements," are shown on the gate of Stirling Castle, page 147. We still use battlements as architectural decorations.

[3] pronounce *varge*

XXX

The offended Monarch rode apart,
With bitter thought and swelling heart, 815
And would not now vouchsafe [1] again
Through Stirling streets to lead his train.
"O Lennox, who would wish to rule
This changeling crowd, this common fool?
Hear'st thou," he said, "the loud acclaim, 820
With which they shout the Douglas name?
With like acclaim, the vulgar throat
Strain'd for King James their morning note;
With like acclaim they hail'd the day
When first I broke the Douglas' sway; 825
And like acclaim would Douglas greet,
If he could hurl me from my seat.
Who o'er the herd would wish to reign,
Fantastic, fickle, fierce, and vain!
Vain as the leaf upon the stream, 830
And fickle as a changeful dream;
Fantastic as a woman's mood,
And fierce as Frenzy's fever'd blood.
Thou many-headed monster-thing,
Oh, who could wish to be thy king! 835

XXXI

"But soft! what messenger of speed
Spurs hitherward his panting steed?
I guess his cognizance [2] afar —
What from our cousin, John of Mar?" — [3]
"He prays, my liege, your sports keep bound 840
Within the safe and guarded ground:
For some foul purpose yet unknown, —
Most sure for evil to the throne, —

---

[1] condescend   [2] his coat of arms   [3] a supporter of the King

The outlaw'd Chieftain, Roderick Dhu,
Has summon'd his rebellious crew;   845
'Tis said, in James of Bothwell's ¹ aid
These loose banditti ² stand array'd.
The Earl of Mar, this morn, from Doune,
To break their muster march'd, and soon
Your grace will hear of battle fought;   850
But earnestly the Earl besought,
Till for such danger he provide,
With scanty train ³ you will not ride."

XXXII

"Thou warn'st me I have done amiss, —
I should have earlier look'd to this: 855
I lost it ⁴ in this bustling day.
— Retrace with speed thy former way;
Spare not for spoiling of thy steed,
The best of mine shall be thy meed.
Say to our faithful Lord of Mar,   860
We do forbid the intended war:
Roderick, this morn, in single fight,
Was made our prisoner by a knight;
And Douglas hath himself and cause
Submitted to our kingdom's laws.   865
The tidings of their leaders lost ⁵
Will soon dissolve the mountain host,
Nor would we that the vulgar ⁶ feel
For their Chief's crimes, avenging steel.
Bear Mar our message, Braco; fly!" —   870
He turn'd his steed, — "My liege, I hie, —
Yet, ere I cross this lily lawn,
I fear the broadswords will be drawn."

---

¹ an enemy of James V   ² robbers   ³ guard, attendants
⁴ I forgot it. What was forgotten?
⁵ news of the loss of their active leaders
⁶ from the Latin *vulgus* meaning "crowd"; hence the common people

The turf the flying courser spurn'd,
And to his towers the King return'd.   875

XXXIII

Ill with King James's mood that day,
Suited gay feast and minstrel lay;
Soon were dismiss'd the courtly throng,
And soon cut short the festal song.
Nor less upon the sadden'd town   880
The evening sunk in sorrow down.
The burghers spoke of civil jar,[1]
Of rumour'd feuds and mountain war,
Of Moray, Mar, and Roderick Dhu,
All up in arms: — the Douglas too,   885
They mourn'd him pent within the hold,[2]
"Where stout Earl William[3] was of old."
And there his word the speaker staid,
And finger on his lip he laid,
Or pointed to his dagger blade.   890
But jaded horsemen, from the west,
At evening to the castle press'd;
And busy talkers said they bore
Tidings of fight on Katrine's shore;
At noon the deadly fray begun,   895
And lasted till the set of sun.
Thus giddy rumour shook the town,
Till closed the Night her pennons brown.[4]

[1] civil war
[2] castle
[3] the eighth Earl of Douglas, who was stabbed by James II in the castle at Stirling
[4] Explain this figure of speech — personification.

CANTO SIXTH

The Guard Room

I

The sun, awakening, through the smoky air
  Of the dark city [1] casts a sullen glance,
Rousing each caitiff [2] to his task of care,
  Of sinful man [3] the sad inheritance;
Summoning revellers from the lagging dance,   5
  Scaring the prowling robber to his den;
Gilding on battled [4] tower the warder's lance,
  And warning student pale to leave his pen,
And yield his drowsy eyes to the kind nurse of men.

What various scenes, and, Oh, what scenes of woe,   10
  Are witness'd by that red and struggling beam!
The fever'd patient, from his pallet low,
  Through crowded hospital beholds its stream;
  The ruin'd maiden trembles at its gleam,
The debtor wakes to thought of gyve [5] and jail,   15
  The love-lorn wretch starts from tormenting dream;
  The wakeful mother, by the glimmering pale,
Trims her sick infant's couch, and soothes his feeble
      wail.

II

At dawn the towers of Stirling rang
With soldier-step and weapon-clang,
While drums, with rolling note, foretell   20
Relief to weary sentinel.
Through narrow loop [6] and casement barr'd,

---

[1] Stirling   [2] wretch   [3] Read Gen. III, 19   [4] embattled
[5] a shackle for the legs
[6] a small opening in the fortifications through which the soldiers shot at the
enemy

The sunbeams sought the Court of Guard,[1]
And, struggling with the smoky air,   25
Deaden'd the torches' yellow glare.
In comfortless alliance shone
The lights through arch of blacken'd stone,
And show'd wild shapes in garb of war,
Faces deform'd with beard and scar,   30
All haggard from the midnight watch,
And fever'd with the stern debauch;[2]
For the oak table's massive board,
Flooded with wine, with fragments stored,
And beakers drain'd, and cups o'erthrown,   35
Show'd in what sport the night had flown.
Some, weary, snored on floor and bench;
Some labour'd still their thirst to quench;
Some, chill'd with watching, spread their hands
O'er the huge chimney's dying brands,   40
While round them, or beside them flung,
At every step their harness[3] rung.

III

These drew not for their fields the sword,
Like tenants of a feudal lord,
Nor own'd the patriarchal claim
Of Chieftain in their leader's name;   45
Adventurers they, from far who roved,
To live by battle which they loved,
There the Italian's clouded face,
The swarthy Spaniard's there you trace;
The mountain-loving Switzer[4] there   50
More freely breathed in mountain-air;
The Fleming[5] there despised the soil,

---

[1] the castle court   [2] intemperance   [3] armor
[4] an inhabitant of Switzerland
[5] a citizen of Flanders, now part of Belgium

That paid so ill the labourer's toil;
Their rolls show'd French and German name;   55
And merry England's exiles came,
To share, with ill-conceal'd disdain,
Of Scotland's pay the scanty gain.
All brave in arms, well train'd to wield
The heavy halberd,[1] brand, and shield;   60
In camps licentious, wild, and bold;
In pillage fierce and uncontroll'd;
And now, by holytide [2] and feast,
From rules of discipline released.

IV

They held debate of bloody fray,   65
Fought 'twixt Loch Katrine and Achray.
Fierce was their speech, and, 'mid their words,
Their hands oft grappled to their swords;
Nor sunk their tone to spare the ear
Of wounded comrades groaning near,   70
Whose mangled limbs, and bodies gored,
Bore token of the mountain sword,
Though, neighbouring to the Court of Guard,
Their prayers and feverish wails were heard;
Sad burden to the ruffian joke,   75
And savage oath by fury spoke! —
At length up-started John of Brent,
A yeoman from the banks of Trent,
A stranger to respect or fear,
In peace a chaser of the deer,   80
In host a hardy mutineer,
But still the boldest of the crew,
When deed of danger was to do.
He grieved, that day, their games cut short,
And marr'd the dicer's brawling sport,   85

----

[1] a kind of broad ax   [2] holiday

And shouted loud, "Renew the bowl!
And, while a merry catch I troll,[1]
Let each the buxom[2] chorus bear,
Like brethren of the brand and spear."

V

Soldier's Song

Our vicar still preaches that Peter and Poule[3]   90
Laid a swinging long curse on the bonny brown bowl,
That there's wrath and despair in the jolly black-
    jack,[4]
And the seven deadly sins in a flagon of sack;
Yet whoop, Barnaby! off with thy liquor,
Drink upsees[5] out, and a fig for the vicar!   95

Our vicar he calls it damnation to sip
The ripe ruddy dew of a woman's dear lip,
Says, that Beelzebub[6] lurks in her kerchief so sly,
And Apollyon[7] shoots darts from her merry black
    eye;
Yet whoop, Jack! kiss Gillian[8] the quicker,   100
Till she bloom like a rose, and a fig for the vicar!

Our vicar thus preaches — and why should he not?
For the dues of his cure[9] are the placket and pot;[10]
And 'tis right of his office poor laymen to lurch,[11]
Who infringe the domains of our good Mother   105
    Church.
Yet whoop, bully-boys! off with your liquor,
Sweet Marjorie's the word, and a fig for the vicar!

[1] to sing loudly
[2] frolicsome
[3] St. Peter and St. Paul
[4] a pitcher made of leather
[5] empty the tankard
[6] a name for Satan
[7] another term for Satan
[8] an old English nickname for Julianna
[9] district, parish
[10] women and ale
[11] to lie in wait

VI

The warder's challenge, heard without,
Staid [1] in mid-roar the merry shout.
A soldier to the portal went, —   110
"Here is old Bertram, sirs, of Ghent;
And, — beat for jubilee the drum!
A maid and minstrel with him come."
Bertram, a Fleming, grey and scarr'd,
Was entering now the Court of Guard,   115
A harper with him, and in plaid
All muffled close, a mountain maid,
Who backward shrunk, to 'scape the view
Of the loose scene and boisterous crew.
"What news?" they roar'd: — "I only know,   120
From noon till eve we fought with foe,
As wild and as untameable
As the rude mountains where they dwell;
On both sides store of blood is lost,
Nor much success can either boast." —   125
"But whence thy captives, friend? such spoil
As theirs must needs reward thy toil.
Old dost thou wax, and wars grow sharp;
Thou now hast glee-maiden [2] and harp!
Get thee an ape, and trudge the land,   130
The leader of a juggler band." —

VII

"No, comrade; — no such fortune mine.
After the fight these sought our line,
That aged harper and the girl,
And, having audience of the Earl,   135

---

[1] stopped
[2] Young girls who accompanied mediæval jugglers and assisted in the entertainment by tumbling, singing, and dancing. This epithet refers to Ellen disrespectfully.

Mar bade I should purvey[1] them steed,
And bring them hitherward with speed.
Forbear your mirth and rude alarm,
For none shall do them shame or harm." —
"Hear ye his boast?" cried John of Brent,   140
Ever to strife and jangling bent;
"Shall he strike doe beside our lodge,
And yet the jealous niggard grudge
To pay the forester his fee?
I'll have my share, howe'er it be,   145
Despite of Moray, Mar, or thee."
Bertram his forward step withstood;
And, burning in his vengeful mood,
Old Allan, though unfit for strife,
Laid hand upon his dagger-knife;   150
But Ellen boldly stepp'd between,
And dropp'd at once the tartan screen: —
So, from his morning cloud, appears
The sun of May, through summer tears.
The savage soldiery, amazed,   155
As on descended angel gazed;
Even hardy Brent, abash'd and tamed,
Stood half admiring, half ashamed.

VIII

Boldly she spoke, — "Soldiers, attend!
My father was the soldier's friend;   160
Cheer'd him in camps, in marches led,
And with him in the battle bled.
Not from the valiant, or the strong,
Should exile's daughter suffer wrong." —
Answer'd De Brent, most forward still   165
In every feat or good or ill, —

---

[1] provide (with horses)

"I shame me [1] of the part I play'd:
And thou an outlaw's child, poor maid!
An outlaw I by forest laws,
And merry Needwood [2] knows the cause.   170
Poor Rose, — if Rose be living now," —
He wiped his iron eye and brow, —
"Must bear such age, I think, as thou.
Hear ye, my mates; — I go to call
The Captain of our watch to hall;   175
There lies my halberd on the floor;
And he that steps my halberd o'er,
To do the maid injurious part,
My shaft shall quiver in his heart! —
Beware loose speech, or jesting rough.   180
Ye all know John de Brent.   Enough."

IX

Their Captain came, a gallant young, —
(Of Tullibardine's house [3] he sprung,)
Nor wore he yet the spurs of knight;
Gay was his mien, his humour light,   185
And, though by courtesy controll'd,
Forward his speech, his bearing bold.
The high-born maiden ill could brook
The scanning of his curious look
And dauntless eye; — and yet, in sooth,   190
Young Lewis was a generous youth;
But Ellen's lovely face and mien,
Ill suited to the garb and scene,
Might lightly bear construction strange,
And give loose fancy scope to range.   195
"Welcome to Stirling towers, fair maid!

[1] I am ashamed. In our older English *shame* was used reflexively.
[2] a royal forest in Staffordshire
[3] the name of the house of the Murray family in Perthshire, about twenty miles from Stirling

THE BRIDGE AT STIRLING
Photo by Ewing Galloway.

Come ye to seek a champion's aid,
On palfrey white, with harper hoar,
Like errant damosel [1] of yore?
Does thy high quest a knight require,   200
Or may the venture suit a squire?" —
Her dark eye flash'd; — she paused and sigh'd, —
"Oh, what have I to do with pride! —
Through scenes of sorrow, shame, and strife,
A suppliant for a father's life,   205
I crave an audience of the King.
Behold, to back my suit, a ring,
The royal pledge of grateful claims,
Given by the Monarch to Fitz-James."

X

The signet-ring young Lewis took,   210
With deep respect and alter'd look;
And said, — "This ring our duties own;
And pardon, if to worth unknown,
In semblance mean obscurely veil'd,
Lady, in aught my folly fail'd.   215
Soon as the day flings wide his gates,
The King shall know what suitor waits.
Please you, meanwhile, in fitting bower [2]
Repose you till his waking hour;
Female attendance shall obey   220
Your hest,[3] for service or array.[4]
Permit I marshal you the way."
But, ere she followed, with the grace
And open bounty of her race,
She bade her slender purse be shared   225
Among the soldiers of the guard.
The rest with thanks their guerdon [5] took;

---

[1] a wandering damsel or maiden   [2] inner chamber   [3] wishes
            [4] dress   [5] reward

But Brent, with shy and awkward look,
On the reluctant maiden's hold
Forced bluntly back the proffer'd gold; —   230
"Forgive a haughty English heart,
And Oh, forget its ruder part!
The vacant purse shall be my share,
Which in my barret-cap [1] I'll bear.
Perchance, in jeopardy of war,   235
Where gayer crests may keep afar."
With thanks, — 'twas all she could — the maid
His rugged courtesy repaid.

XI

When Ellen forth with Lewis went,
Allan made suit to John of Brent: —   240
"My lady safe, O let your grace
Give me to see my master's face! [2]
His minstrel I, — to share his doom
Bound from the cradle to the tomb.
Tenth in descent, since first my sires   245
Waked for his noble house their lyres,
Nor one of all the race was known
But prized its weal [3] above their own.
With the Chief's birth begins our care;
Our harp must soothe the infant heir,   250
Teach the youth tales of fight, and grace
His earliest feat of field or chase;
In peace, in war, our rank we keep,
We cheer his board, we soothe his sleep,
Nor leave him till we pour our verse, —   255
A doleful tribute! — o'er his hearse,
Then let me share his captive lot;

---

[1] a flat cap formerly worn by soldiers
[2] the face of Douglas. John of Brent believes he means Roderick's.
[3] welfare

It is my right — deny it not!" —
"Little we reck," [1] said John of Brent,
"We Southern men, of long descent;   260
Nor wot [2] we how a name — a word —
Makes clansmen vassals to a lord:
Yet kind my noble landlord's part, —
God bless the house of Beaudesert! [3]
And, but I loved to drive the deer,   265
More than to guide the labouring steer,
I had not dwelt an outcast here.
Come, good old Minstrel, follow me;
Thy Lord and Chieftain shalt thou see."

XII

Then, from a rusted iron hook,   270
A bunch of ponderous keys he took,
Lighted a torch, and Allan led
Through grated arch and passage dread.
Portals they pass'd, where, deep within,
Spoke prisoner's moan, and fetters' din;   275
Through rugged vaults, where, loosely stored,
Lay wheel, and axe,[4] and headsman's sword,
And many a hideous engine grim,
For wrenching joint, and crushing limb,
By artist form'd, who deem'd it shame   280
And sin to give their work a name.
They halted at a low brow'd porch,
And Brent to Allan gave the torch,
While bolt and chain he backward roll'd,
And made the bar unhasp [5] its hold.   285
They enter'd: — 'twas a prison-room
Of stern security and gloom,

[1] care   [2] know
[3] the house of his former landlord
[4] The wheel and axle were used for torturing people.
[5] unloose

Yet not a dungeon; for the day
Through lofty gratings found its way,
And rude and antique garniture [1]   290
Deck'd the sad walls and oaken floor;
Such as the rugged days of old
Deem'd fit for captive noble's hold. [2]
"Here," said De Brent, "thou mayst remain
Till the Leech [3] visit him again.   295
Strict is his charge, the warders tell,
To tend the noble prisoner well."
Retiring then the bolt he drew,
And the lock's murmurs growl'd anew.
Roused at the sound, from lowly bed   300
A captive feebly raised his head;
The wondering Minstrel look'd, and knew —
Not his dear lord, but Roderick Dhu!
For, come from where Clan-Alpine fought,
They, erring, deem'd the Chief he sought.   305

XIII

As the tall ship, whose lofty prore [4]
Shall never stem the billows more,
Deserted by her gallant band,
Amid the breakers lies astrand, — [5]
So, on his couch, lay Roderick Dhu!   310
And oft his fever'd limbs he threw
In toss abrupt, as when her sides
Lie rocking in the advancing tides,
That shake her frame with ceaseless beat,
Yet cannot heave her from her seat; —   315
Oh, how unlike her course at sea!
Or his free step on hill and lea! —
Soon as the Minstrel he could scan,

---

[1] ancient furnishings   [2] a prison where nobility was confined
          [3] physician   [4] prow   [5] stranded

— "What of thy lady? — tell me all,
Have they been ruin'd in my fall?   320
Ah, yes! or wherefore art thou here!
Yet speak, — speak boldly, — do not fear." —
(For Allan, who his mood well knew,
Was choked with grief and terror too.)
"Who fought — who fled? — Old man, be brief; —325
Some might — for they had lost their Chief.
Who basely live? — who bravely died?"
"Oh, calm thee, Chief!" the Minstrel cried,
"Ellen is safe;" — "For that thank Heaven!" —
"And hopes are for the Douglas given; —   330
The Lady Margaret too is well;
And, for thy clan, — on field or fell,
Has never harp of minstrel told,
Of combat fought so true and bold.
Thy stately Pine is yet unbent,   335
Though many a goodly bough is rent."

XIV

The Chieftain rear'd his form on high,
And fever's fire was in his eye;
But ghastly pale, and livid streaks
Chequer'd his swarthy brow and cheeks.   340
— "Hark, Minstrel!   I have heard thee play,
With measure bold, on festal day,
In yon lone isle, . . . again where ne'er
Shall harper play, or warrior hear! . . .
That stirring air that peals on high,   345
O'er Dermid's race our victory. —
Strike it! — and then (for well thou canst),
Free from thy minstrel spirit glanced.
Fling me the picture of the fight
When met my clan the Saxon might.   350
I'll listen, till my fancy hears

The clang of swords, the crash of spears!
These grates, these walls, shall vanish then,
For the fair field of fighting men,
And my free spirit burst away,   355
As if it soar'd from battle fray." [1]
The trembling Bard with awe obey'd, —
Slow on the harp his hand he laid;
But soon remembrance of the sight
He witness'd from the mountain's height,   360
With what old Bertram told at night,
Awaken'd the full power of song,
And bore him in career along; —
As shallop launch'd on river's tide,
That slow and fearful leaves the side,   365
But, when it feels the middle stream,
Drives downward swift as lightning's beam.

XV

Battle of Beal' an Duine [2]

"The Minstrel came once more to view
The eastern ridge of Ben Venue,
For ere he parted, he would say   370
Farewell to lovely Loch Achray —
Where shall he find in foreign land,
So lone a lake, so sweet a strand!
   There is no breeze upon the fern,
     Nor ripple on the lake,   375
Upon her eyry nods the erne, [3]
    The deer has sought the brake;

[1] Roderick loved this song so much he expressed a desire to hear it on his death bed.

[2] "A skirmish actually took place at a pass thus called in the Trossachs, and closed with the remarkable incident mentioned in the text. It was greatly posterior in date to the reign of James V." Scott.

[3] eagle

The small birds will not sing aloud,
   The springing trout lies still,
So darkly glooms yon thunder cloud,   380
That swathes, as with a purple shroud,
   Ben Ledi's distant hill.
Is it the thunder's solemn sound
   That mutters deep and dread,
Or echoes from the groaning ground   385
   The warrior's measured tread?
Is it the lightning's quivering glance
   That on the thicket streams,
Or do they flash on spear and lance
   The sun's retiring beams? —   390
I see the dagger-crest of Mar,
I see the Moray's silver star,
Wave o'er the cloud of Saxon war,
That up the lake comes winding far!
   To hero bound for battle-strife,   395
      Or bard of martial lay,
  'Twere worth ten years of peaceful life,
      One glance at their array!

XVI

"Their light-arm'd archers far and near
   Survey'd the tangled ground,   400
Their centre ranks, with pike and spear,
   A twilight forest frown'd,
Their barbed [1] horsemen, in the rear,
   The stern battalia [2] crown'd.
No cymbal clash'd, no clarion rang,   405
   Still were the pipe and drum;
Save heavy tread, and armour's clang,
   The sullen march was dumb.

---

[1] armored
[2] The line of battle

There breathed no wind their crests to shake,
  Or wave their flags abroad;   410
Scarce the frail aspen seem'd to quake,
  That shadow'd o'er their road.
Their vaward [1] scouts no tidings bring,
  Can rouse no lurking foe,
Nor spy a trace of living thing,   415
    Save when they stirr'd the roe;
  The host moves, like a deep-sea wave,
  Where rise no rocks its pride to brave,
    High-swelling, dark, and slow.
The lake is pass'd, and now they gain   420
A narrow and a broken plain,
Before the Trossachs' rugged jaws;
And here the horse and spearmen pause,
While, to explore the dangerous glen,
Dive through the pass the archer-men.   425

XVII

"At once there rose so wild a yell
Within that dark and narrow dell,
As all the fiends, from heaven that fell,
Had peal'd the banner-cry of hell!
Forth from the pass in tumult driven,   430
Like chaff before the wind of heaven,
  The archery [2] appear:
For life! for life! their plight they ply — [3]
And shriek, and shout, and battle-cry,
And plaids and bonnets waving high,   435
And broadswords flashing to the sky,
  Are maddening in the rear.
Onward they drive, in dreadful race,
  Pursuers and pursued;
Before that tide of flight and chase,   440

---

[1] vanguard   [2] archers   [3] They engage in battle.

How shall it keep its rooted place,
    The spearmen's twilight wood? —
'Down, down,' cried Mar, 'your lances down!
    Bear back both friend and foe!' —
Like reeds before the tempest's frown,   445
That serried grove of lances brown
    At once lay levell'd low;
And closely shouldering side to side,
The bristling ranks the onset bide. —
'We'll quell the savage mountaineer,   450
    As their Tinchel [1] cows the game!
They come as fleet as forest deer,
    We'll drive them back as tame.' —

XVIII

"Bearing before them, in their course,
The relics of the archer force,   455
Like wave with crest of sparkling foam,
Right onward did Clan-Alpine come.
    Above the tide, each broadsword bright,
    Was brandishing like beam of light,
        Each targe was dark below;   460
    And with the ocean's mighty swing,
    When heaving to the tempest's wing,
        They hurl'd them on the foe.
I heard the lance's shivering crash,
As when the whirlwind rends the ash;   465
I heard the broadsword's deadly clang,
As if an hundred anvils rang!
But Moray wheel'd his rearward rank
Of horsemen on Clan-Alpine's flank,
    — 'My banner-man, advance!   470

---

[1] "A circle of sportsmen, by surrounding a great space, and gradually narrowing, brought immense quantities of deer together, which usually made desperate efforts to break through the *Tinchel*."   Scott.

I see,' he cried, 'their column shake. —
Now, gallants! for your ladies' sake,
  Upon them with the lance!' —
The horsemen dash'd among the rout,
  As deer break through the broom;   475
Their steeds are stout, their swords are out,
  They soon make lightsome room.
Clan-Alpine's best are backward borne —
  Where, where was Roderick then!
One blast upon his bugle-horn   480
  Were worth a thousand men.
And refluent [1] through the pass of fear
  The battle's tide was pour'd;
Vanish'd the Saxon's struggling spear,
  Vanish'd the mountain-sword.   485
As Bracklinn's chasm, so black and steep,
  Receives her roaring linn, [2]
As the dark caverns of the deep
  Suck the wild whirlpool in,
So did the deep and darksome pass   490
Devour the battle's mingled mass:
None linger now upon the plain,
Save those who ne'er shall fight again.

XIX

"Now westward rolls the battle's din,
That deep and doubling pass within,   495
— Minstrel, away! the work of fate
Is bearing on; its issue wait,
Where the rude Trossachs' dread defile
Opens on Katrine's lake and isle. —
Grey Ben Venue I soon repass'd,   500
Loch Katrine lay beneath me cast.

---

    [1] ebbing, flowing back   [2] cataract

The sun is set, — the clouds are met,
   The lowering scowl of heaven
  An inky hue of livid blue
    To the deep lake has given;   505
Strange gusts of wind from mountain-glen
Swept o'er the lake, then sunk agen.
I heeded not the eddying surge,
Mine eye but saw the Trossachs' gorge,
Mine ear but heard the sullen sound,   510
Which like an earthquake shook the ground,
And spoke the stern and desperate strife
That parts not but with parting life,
Seeming, to minstrel ear, to toll
The dirge of many a passing soul.   515
Nearer it comes — the dim-wood glen
The martial flood disgorged agen,
  But not in mingled tide;
The plaided warriors of the North
High on the mountain thunder forth   520
  And overhang its side;
While by the lake below appears
The dark'ning cloud of Saxon spears.
At weary bay each shatter'd band,
Eyeing their foemen, sternly stand;   525
Their banners stream like tatter'd sail,
That flings its fragments to the gale,
And broken arms and disarray
Mark'd the fell havoc of the day.

XX

"Viewing the mountain's ridge askance,   530
The Saxon stood in sullen trance,
Till Moray pointed with his lance,
   And cried — 'Behold yon isle! —

See! none are left to guard its strand,
But women weak, that wring the hand: 535
'Tis there of yore the robber band
     Their booty wont to pile; —
My purse, with bonnet-pieces [1] store,
To him will swim [2] a bow-shot o'er,
And loose a shallop from the shore.   540
Lightly we'll tame the war-wolf then,
Lords of his mate, and brood, and den.'
Forth from the ranks a spearman sprung,
On earth his casque [3] and corselet [4] rung,
     He plunged him in the wave: —   545
All saw the deed — the purpose knew,
And to their clamours Ben Venue
     A mingled echo gave;
The Saxons shout, their mate to cheer,
The helpless females scream for fear,   550
And yells for rage the mountaineer.
'Twas then, as by the outcry riven,
Pour'd down at once the lowering heaven;
A whirlwind swept Loch Katrine's breast,
Her billows rear'd their snowy crest.   555
Well for the swimmer swell'd they high,
To mar the Highland marksman's eye;
For round him shower'd, 'mid rain and hail,
The vengeful arrows of the Gael. —
In vain — He nears the isle — and lo!   560
His hand is on a shallop's bow.
— Just then a flash of lightning came,
It tinged the waves and strand with flame: —
I mark'd Duncraggan's widow'd dame,[5]

---

[1] "A gold coin on which the king's head was represented with a bonnet instead of a crown, coined by the 'Commons' King.'" Taylor.
[2] to him who will swim   [3] helmet
[4] armor for the protection of the front of the body
[5] Reread XVIII, Canto III.

Behind an oak I saw her stand,   565
A naked dirk gleam'd in her hand: —
It darken'd, — but, amid the moan
Of waves, I heard a dying groan; —
Another flash! — the spearman floats
A weltering corse [1] beside the boats,   570
And the stern matron o'er him stood,
Her hand and dagger streaming blood.

XXI

" 'Revenge! revenge!' the Saxons cried,
The Gaels' exulting shout replied.
Despite the elemental rage,   575
Again they hurried to engage;
But, ere they closed in desperate fight,
Bloody with spurring came a knight,
Sprung from his horse, and, from a crag,
Waved 'twixt the hosts a milk-white flag.   580
Clarion and trumpet by his side
Rung forth a truce-note high and wide,
While, in the Monarch's name, afar
An herald's voice forbade the war,
For Bothwell's lord, and Roderick bold,   585
Were both, he said, in captive hold."
— But here the lay made sudden stand,
The harp escaped the Minstrel's hand! —
Oft had he stolen a glance, to spy
How Roderick brook'd [2] his minstrelsy: 590
At first, the Chieftain, to the chime,
With lifted hand, kept feeble time;
That motion ceased, — yet feeling strong
Varied his look as changed the song;
At length, no more his deafen'd ear   595
The minstrel melody can hear;

---

[1] a bloody body   [2] received

His face grows sharp, — his hands are clench'd,
As if some pang his heart-strings wrench'd;
Set are his teeth, his fading eye
Is sternly fix'd on vacancy;   600
Thus, motionless, and moanless, drew
His parting breath, stout Roderick Dhu! —
Old Allan-bane look'd on aghast,
While grim and still his spirit pass'd;
But when he saw that life was fled,   605
He pour'd his wailing o'er the dead.

XXII

Lament

"And art thou cold and lowly laid,
Thy foeman's dread, thy people's aid,
Breadalbane's boast, Clan-Alpine's shade!
For thee shall none a requiem [1] say?   610
— For thee, — who loved the minstrel's lay,
For thee, of Bothwell's house the stay,
The shelter of her exiled line,
E'en in this prison-house of thine
I'll wail for Alpine's honour'd Pine!   615

"What groans shall yonder valleys fill!
What shrieks of grief shall rend yon hill!
What tears of burning rage shall thrill,
When mourns thy tribe thy battles done,
Thy fall before the race was won,   620
Thy sword ungirt ere set of sun!
There breathes not clansman of thy line,
But would have given his life for thine. —
Oh, woe for Alpine's honour'd Pine!

[1] a hymn or mass sung for the repose of the soul after death

"Sad was thy lot on mortal stage! —   625
The captive thrush may brook the cage,
The prison'd eagle dies for rage.
Brave spirit, do not scorn my strain!
And, when its notes awake again,
Even she, so long beloved in vain,   630
Shall with my harp her voice combine,
And mix her woe and tears with mine,
To wail Clan-Alpine's honour'd Pine." —

XXIII

Ellen, the while, with bursting heart,
Remain'd in lordly bower apart,   635
Where play'd, with many colour'd gleams,
Through storied pane [1] the rising beams.
In vain on gilded roof they fall,
And lighten'd up a tapestried wall
And for her use a menial train [2]   640
A rich collation [3] spread in vain.
The banquet proud, the chamber gay,
Scarce drew one curious glance astray;
Or if she look'd, 'twas but to say,
With better omen dawn'd the day   645
In that lone isle, where waved on high
The dun-deer's hide for canopy;
Where oft her noble father shared
The simple meal her care prepared,
While Lufra, crouching by her side,   650
Her station claim'd with jealous pride,
And Douglas, bent on woodland game,
Spoke of the chase to Malcolm Graeme,
Whose answer, oft at random made,
The wandering of his thoughts betray'd. —   655

---

[1] adorned with historical or Biblical stories
[2] a train of servants   [3] feast

Those who such simple joys have known,
Are taught to prize them when they're gone.
But sudden, see, she lifts her head!
The window seeks with cautious tread.
What distant music has the power   660
To win her in this woeful hour!
'Twas from a turret that o'erhung
Her latticed bower, the strain was sung.

XXIV

Lay of the Imprisoned Huntsman

"My hawk is tired of perch and hood,
My idle greyhound loathes his food,   665
My horse is weary of his stall,
And I am sick of captive thrall.
I wish I were as I have been,
Hunting the hart in forest green,
With bended bow and bloodhound free,   670
For that's the life is meet for me.
I hate to learn the ebb of time,
From yon dull steeple's drowsy chime,
Or mark it as the sunbeams crawl,
Inch after inch, along the wall.   675
The lark was wont my matins ring,
The sable rook my vespers sing;
These towers, although a king's they be,
Have not a hall of joy for me.
No more at dawning morn I rise,   680
And sun myself in Ellen's eyes,
Drive the fleet deer the forest through,
And homeward wend with evening dew;
A blithesome welcome blithely meet,
And lay my trophies at her feet,   685
While fled the eve on wing of glee, —
That life is lost to love and me!"

XXV

The heart-sick lay was hardly said,
The list'ner had not turn'd her head,
It trickled still, the starting tear, 690
When light a footstep struck her ear,
And Snowdoun's graceful knight was near.
She turn'd the hastier, lest again
The prisoner should renew his strain.
"O welcome, brave Fitz-James!" she said; 695
"How may an almost orphan maid
Pay the deep debt?" — "Oh, say not so!
To me no gratitude you owe.
Not mine, alas! the boon [1] to give,
And bid thy noble father live; 700
I can but be thy guide, sweet maid,
With Scotland's King thy suit to aid.
No tyrant he, though ire and pride
May lay his better mood aside.
Come, Ellen, come! 'tis more than time, 705
He holds his court at morning prime."
With beating heart, and bosom wrung,
As to a brother's arm she clung.
Gently he dried the falling tear,
And gently whisper'd hope and cheer; 710
Her faltering steps, half led, half staid,
Through gallery fair, and high arcade,
Till, at his touch, its wings of pride
A portal arch unfolded wide.

XXVI

Within 'twas brilliant all and light, 715
A thronging scene of figures bright;

[1] blessing

It glow'd on Ellen's dazzled sight,
As when the setting sun has given
Ten thousand hues to summer even,
And from their tissue, fancy frames   720
Aerial knights and fairy dames.
Still by Fitz-James her footing staid; [1]
A few faint steps she forward made,
Then slow her drooping head she raised,
And fearful round the presence gazed;   725
For him she sought, who own'd this state,
The dreaded Prince whose will was fate! —
She gazed on many a princely port,
Might well have ruled a royal court;
On many a splendid garb she gazed, —   730
Then turn'd bewildered and amazed,
For all stood bare; and, in the room,
Fitz-James alone wore cap and plume.
To him each lady's look was lent;
On him each courtier's eye was bent;   735
Midst furs and silks and jewels sheen,
He stood, in simple Lincoln green,
The centre of the glittering ring, —
And Snowdoun's Knight is Scotland's King.

XXVII

As wreath of snow, on mountain-breast,   740
Slides from the rock that gave it rest,
Poor Ellen glided from her stay,
And at the Monarch's feet she lay;
No word her choking voice commands, —
She show'd the ring — she clasped her hands.   745
Oh, not a moment could he brook,
The generous Prince, that suppliant look!

[1] lingered

Gently he raised her, — and, the while,
Check'd with a glance the circle's smile;
Graceful, but grave, her brow he kiss'd,   750
And bade her terrors be dismiss'd: —
"Yes, Fair; the wandering poor Fitz-James
The fealty of Scotland claims.
To him thy woes, thy wishes, bring;
He will redeem his signet ring.   755
Ask nought for Douglas; — yester even,[1]
His prince and he have much forgiven.
Wrong hath he had from slanderous tongue,
I, from his rebel kinsmen, wrong.
We would not, to the vulgar crowd,   760
Yield what they craved with clamour loud;
Calmly we heard and judged his cause,
Our council aided, and our laws.
I stanch'd thy father's death-feud stern,
With Stout De Vaux and Grey Glencairn;   765
And Bothwell's lord henceforth we own
The friend and bulwark of our Throne. —
But, lovely infidel, how now?
What clouds thy misbelieving brow?
Lord James of Douglas, lend thine aid;   770
Thou must confirm this doubting maid."

XXVIII

Then forth the noble Douglas sprung,
And on his neck his daughter hung.
The Monarch drank, that happy hour,
The sweetest, holiest draught of Power, —   775
When it can say, with godlike voice,
Arise, sad Virtue, and rejoice!
Yet would not James the general eye
On Nature's raptures long should pry;

[1] yesterday evening

He stepp'd between — "Nay, Douglas, nay,   780
Steal not my proselyte away!
The riddle 'tis my right to read,
That brought this happy chance to speed.
— Yes, Ellen, when disguised I stray
In life's more low but happier way,   785
'Tis under name which veils my power,
Nor falsely veils — for Stirling's tower
Of yore the name of Snowdoun claims,
And Normans call me James Fitz-James.[1]
Thus watch I o'er insulted laws,   790
Thus learn to right the injured cause." —
Then, in a tone apart and low, —
"Ah, little traitress! none must know
What idle dream, what lighter thought,
What vanity full dearly bought,   795
Join'd to thine eye's dark witchcraft, drew
My spell-bound steps to Ben Venue,
In dangerous hour, and all but gave
Thy Monarch's life to mountain glaive!" —
Aloud he spoke — "Thou still dost hold   800
That little talisman of gold, [2]
Pledge of my faith, Fitz-James's ring —
What seeks fair Ellen of the King?"

XXIX

Full well the conscious maiden guess'd
He probed the weakness of her breast;   805
But, with that consciousness, there came
A lightening of her fears for Graeme,
And more she deem'd the Monarch's ire
Kindled 'gainst him, who, for her sire
Rebellious broadsword boldly drew;   810
And, to her generous feeling true,

---

[1] He explains his right to bear both names.   [2] the ring of Fitz-James

She craved the grace of Roderick Dhu.
"Forbear thy suit: — the King of kings
Alone can stay life's parting wings,
I know his heart, I know his hand,   815
Have shared his cheer, and proved his brand: —
My fairest earldom would I give
To bid Clan-Alpine's Chieftain live! —
Hast thou no other boon to crave?
No other captive friend to save?"   820
Blushing, she turn'd her from the King,
And to the Douglas gave the ring,
As if she wish'd her sire to speak
The suit that stain'd [1] her glowing cheek. —
"Nay, then, my pledge has lost its force,   825
And stubborn justice holds her course. —
Malcolm, come forth!" — and, at the word,
Down kneel'd the Graeme to Scotland's Lord.
"For thee, rash youth, no suppliant sues,
From thee may Vengeance claim her dues,   830
Who, nurtur'd underneath our smile,
Hast paid our care by treacherous wile, [2]
And sought, amid thy faithful clan,
A refuge for an outlaw'd man,
Dishonouring thus thy loyal name. —   835
Fetters and warder for the Graeme!" —
His chain of gold the King unstrung,
The links o'er Malcolm's neck he flung,
Then gently drew the glittering band,
And laid the clasp on Ellen's hand.   840

Harp of the North, farewell! The hills grow dark,
    On purple peaks a deeper shade descending;
In twilight copse the glow-worm lights her spark,
    The deer, half-seen, are to the covert wending.

     [1] flushed   [2] a plot for the betrayal of a trust

Resume thy wizard elm! [1] the fountain lending,   845
  And the wild breeze, thy wilder minstrelsy;
Thy numbers sweet with nature's vespers blending,
  With distant echo from the fold and lea,
And herd-boy's evening pipe, and hum of housing
    bee.

Yet, once again, farewell, thou Minstrel harp!   850
  Yet, once again, forgive my feeble sway,
And little reck [2] I of the censure sharp
  May idly cavil at [3] an idle lay.
Much have I owed thy strains on life's long way,
  Through secret woes the world has never known, 855
When on the weary night dawn'd wearier day,
  And bitterer was the grief devour'd alone.
That I o'erlived such woes, Enchantress! is thine
    own.

Hark! as my lingering footsteps slow retire,
  Some Spirit of the Air has waked thy string!   860
'Tis now a seraph [4] bold, with touch of fire,
  'Tis now the brush of Fairy's frolic wing.
Receding now, the dying numbers ring
  Fainter and fainter down the rugged dell,
And now the mountain breezes scarcely bring   865
  A wandering witch-note of the distant spell —
And now, 'tis silent all! — Enchantress, fare thee
    well!

---

[1] Reread in the opening lines about the witch elm.
[2] care
[3] find fault
[4] angel

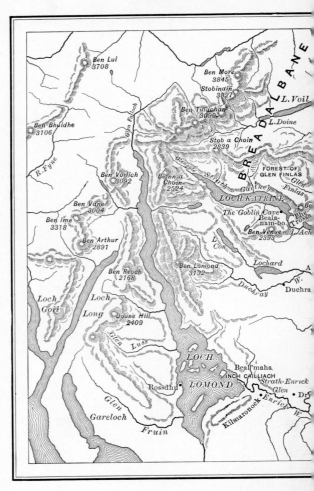

MAP OF THE SCENE OF

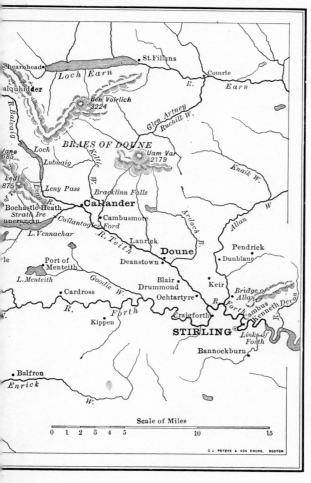

Chearnhead • • St.Fillans
Loch Earn • Comrie
alquhidder R. Earn
Ben Voirlich
3224
R. Balvaig Glen Artney
Ruchill W.
lane *BRAES OF DOUNE*
685 Uam Var
Loch 2179
Lubnaig Knaik W.
edi *Leny Pass* W.
875 Bracklinn Falls
Bochastle Heath **Callander**
Strath Ire • Cambusmore
uncraggan Coillantogle Ford Ardoch B. Allan
L.Vennachar R. Teith Lanrick
le Port of **Doune** • Pendrick
Menteith Deanstown • Dunblane
L.Menteith Goodie W. Blair • Keir
• Cardross Drummond • Bridge of
Ochtartyre • Allan
R. Craigforth Cambus kenneth Dercn
Forth **STIRLING** • Links of
Kippen Forth
Bannockburn
• Balfron
Enrick
W.

Scale of Miles

0 1 2 3 4 5   10   15

C J PETERS & SON ENGRS. BOSTON

HE LADY OF THE LAKE"

APPENDIX I

QUESTIONS AND PROJECTS

CANTO I

I. GEOGRAPHICAL.

1. Draw a map of the land of *The Lady of the Lake*, and on it show the location of all places mentioned in this canto. 2. On this map draw a line showing the course of the stag and the hunter.

II. HISTORICAL.

1. Write a sketch of the reign of James V. 2. Why did the king participate in the chase? 3. Are the characters in this canto true to history? 4. Inasmuch as Ellen and Roderick were cousins, would the law have permitted their marriage?

III. EXPLANATIONS.

1. Give meanings of the following: *Trossachs, reveille, grisly, Lincoln green, canto, sheen, witch-elm, Harp of the North, Uam-Var, rill.* 2. What is meant by the "rocky isle"? 3. Why was James Fitz-James called the "Knight of Snowdoun"? 4. Is there any reason why he should call himself "James Fitz-James"? Look up the word "Fitz" in the dictionary. 5. Make a list of five obsolete words found in this canto. 6. Explain: "My hope, my heaven, my trust must be, my gentle guide, in following thee!"

IV. TO MEMORIZE.

1. Memorize the first stanza of the chase. 2. Commit to memory the song found in stanza XXXI.

V. ORAL OR WRITTEN COMPOSITION.

1. Give oral or written compositions using the following topics: (*a*) A Character Sketch or Study of Ellen and Fitz-James, (*b*) Ellen's Isle, (*c*) The Hunter's Dream, (*d*) The Stag Hunt, (*e*) The Trossachs.

VI. GENERAL.

1. Summarize the story of the first canto. 2. Why did Ellen and Dame Margaret conceal their identity? 3. Give a description of

the Lady of the Lake when Fitz-James first met her. 4. How does Scott make use of "onomatopœia"? 5. A series of paintings could be made to illustrate the events of this canto. Suggest each picture, and tell what it should contain. 6. What is the difference between prose and poetry? 7. What can you say about the meter of this poem? 8. Give reasons for the introduction of archaic words. 9. Reread stanzas XI–XIV for their descriptions of natural scenery; and XVII–XIX and XXI for character descriptions. 10. Mention three incidents that attracted your attention in this canto.

CANTO II

I. GEOGRAPHICAL.

1. Draw a map of Loch Katrine, and on it locate Ellen's Isle. (Do not mispronounce the word "Katrine.") 2. Who inhabited this rocky islet? 3. Give approximately the distance between Ellen's Isle and the silver strand.

II. HISTORICAL.

1. Relate the story of the famous Douglas family. 2. Why were Ellen and her father in exile? 3. Are these characters true to history? Give proofs.

III. EXPLANATIONS.

1. Explain the following: "minstrel gray," "tuneful fathers," "Bothwell's bannered hall," "Ere Douglases to ruin driven," "Percy's Norman pennon." 2. Give meanings of *nighted, streight, unhooded, henchman, reave.* 3. What is meant by "Such cheek should feel the midnight air"? 4. What and where is the Holy-Rood?

IV. TO MEMORIZE.

1. Memorize the boat song. 2. Commit to memory the last twelve lines of this canto.

V. ORAL OR WRITTEN COMPOSITION.

1. Assume that you have visited Ellen's Isle. Write a letter to your parents describing this famous island in Loch Katrine. 2. Write outlines for themes on the following topics: (*a*) The Return of the Clan Alpine, (*b*) Sir Roderick's Proposal to the Douglas, (*c*) The Use of the Falcon in Hunting.

VI. GENERAL.

1. Summarize the events in this canto. 2. Give character sketches of Allan-bane, Malcolm, Douglas, and Roderick Dhu.

3. What can you say of the meter of the songs? 4. What prompted Douglas to retire to a neighboring cave? 5. Account for the fact that Sir Roderick Dhu received Malcolm Graeme with stately hospitality. 6. Make a list of quotations from this canto in which human passions are displayed. 7. Give a mental picture of the aged harper, Allan-bane. 8. What was the Fiery Cross? 9. Make a list of fifty words that can be used for a spelling lesson. 10. If you were planning to dramatize this canto, what events should you select? What scenery would be needed?

CANTO III

I. GEOGRAPHICAL.

1. On your map locate Goblin Cave. 2. In your scrapbook draw an outline map showing the Loch Katrine district. Trace the progress of the signal to Duncraggan, through the Pass of Leny, to the Chapel of Saint Bride, by the side of Loch Lubnaig, through Balquidder, Glenfinlas, and Strath-Gartney. 3. Give a description of (a) Ben Ledi, (b) Loch Voil, (c) Coir-Uriskin.

II. HISTORICAL.

1. Show how superstition played an important part in the border warfare. 2. In this canto did Scott deviate from history? Explain. 3. What can you say about "foraging expeditions"? 4. Select a member of your class to refer to "Scott's notes" for information concerning the progress of the signal through the lake and mountain districts. 5. Describe the shepherd custom of burning the dead herbage in the autumn or spring.

III. EXPLANATIONS.

1. Give meanings of the following: *strath, River Demon, cubit, dun deer's hide, Ave Maria.* 2. Explain: (a) "Time rolls his ceaseless course," (b) "The lark sent down her revelry," (c) "Ben Ledi saw the Cross of Fire," (d) "And Silence claimed her evening reign."

IV. TO MEMORIZE.

1. Memorize "Ave Maria." 2. Name other stanzas that should be memorized.

V. ORAL OR WRITTEN COMPOSITION.

1. Write themes on the following topics: (a) The Gathering, (b) How the Clansmen Were Notified of the Meeting. 2. Prepare an oral talk on "Life in the Goblin Cave." 3. Write a character

sketch of Brian. 4. Make outlines for the following: (*a*) Roderick Dhu as a Leader, (*b*) Superstition, (*c*) The Fiery Cross, (*d*) Ave Maria.

VI. GENERAL.

1. Write a summary of this canto. 2. What was the main purpose of the gathering? 3. Tell all you can about Malise's race. 4. Name any relics of an ancient practice you may have found in this canto. 5. Did you notice the number of archaic words? Is the poet justified in using them? 6. What can you say about the meter of the songs? 7. Name all the carriers of the Fiery Cross. 8. Give a complete story of the Fiery Cross, using the following outline: (*a*) Purpose, (*b*) Preparation, (*c*) Journey, (*d*) Response.

CANTO IV

I. GEOGRAPHICAL.

1. On your map locate all the places mentioned in this canto. 2. Describe the Aurora Borealis. What causes it? What is the name of this phenomenon in the regions south of the equator?

II. HISTORICAL.

1. Read Scott for information about the Taghairm. 2. Select a member of your class to read Stevenson's *Kidnapped*, especially observing Highland hospitality.

III. EXPLANATIONS.

1. Give meanings of *mavis, vair, bourne, weeds, solstice*. 2. Explain: (*a*) "Fatal green," (*b*) "Forth it shall," (*c*) "The toils are pitched," (*d*) "A stag of ten," (*e*) "Pound his eyes."

IV. TO MEMORIZE.

1. Memorize the first stanza of "The Prophecy." 2. Make a list of three other passages that should be memorized.

V. ORAL OR WRITTEN COMPOSITION.

1. Use the following topics for either oral or written composition: (*a*) Blanche of Devon, (*b*) The Hospitality of the Highlanders, (*c*) The Music of the Harp, (*d*) The Second Visit of Fitz-James, (*e*) The Prophecy: What was it? Who made it? To whom was it made?

VI. GENERAL.

1. Summarize Canto IV. 2. Why did Roderick resort to the Taghairm? 3. Tell Murdoch's part in this canto. 4. Give reasons for Scott's introduction of the ballad. 5. From this ballad select a number of choice expressions that help us to form clear pictures. 6. Mention the traits in Ellen's character which you have observed from the beginning of the poem.

CANTO V

I. GEOGRAPHICAL.

1. Locate on your map Coilantogle Ford. How far is it from Callander? 2. Find the lines in the poem that describe the scene of the combat. 3. Name and describe the three parent lakes.

II. HISTORICAL.

1. Explain the causes of the feuds between the Lowlanders and Highlanders. 2. What is meant by the reference to Rome's empire? 3. What evidences are there that an old Roman camp stood here at one time? 4. Do you think this combat is historically true?

III. EXPLANATIONS.

1. Interpret: "Thus Fate hath solved her prophecy, Then yield to Fate, and not to me." 2. Explain the following quotation: "Shine martial Faith, and Courtesy's bright star!" 3. What does this expression mean, "thou many-headed monster thing"? 4. Give meanings of *truncheon, pilgrim, squires, bride of heaven, morrice-dancers*.

IV. TO MEMORIZE.

1. Memorize the first stanza of "The Combat."

V. ORAL OR WRITTEN COMPOSITION.

1. Prepare oral or written compositions on the following topics: (*a*) A Visit to Coilantogle, (*b*) The Sports at Stirling, (*c*) The Challenge and Reply, (*d*) The Combat, (*e*) On the Way to Stirling, (*f*) The Outlaw and His King, (*g*) The Message of Intended Battle, (*h*) The Coming of Sorrowful Evening, (*i*) Scott as a Horseman, (*j*) Robin Hood.

VI. GENERAL.

1. Give a synopsis of this canto. 2. Procure the necessary pictures to illustrate the scenes of this canto. Be prepared to talk

about each. 3. Select the most interesting incident in this canto and give reasons for your decision. 4. What means did Scott use in showing the speed of the ride of Fitz-James? 5. Which appeals to you most in the poem — nature study, dramatic incidents, romance, or character drawing? Explain. 6. Give the causes and results of the combat between James Fitz-James and Roderick Dhu. 7. Read Browning's "How They Brought the Good News from Ghent to Aix." Also read Longfellow's "Paul Revere's Ride." 8. Why do scholars consider this canto the most brilliant and thrilling in the poem? 9. Concerning games read Homer (Pope's Translation), *Iliad* XXIII; Virgil (Conington's Translation), *Æneid* V; Milton, *Paradise Lost*, II, 506–569. 10. What are the qualifications of a good athlete? 11. Name some outstanding athletes of the world, beginning with those mentioned in the Bible.

CANTO VI

I. GEOGRAPHICAL.

1. On your map locate Stirling. Describe all scenes mentioned by the author. 2. Locate Trent River, Staffordshire, Tullibardine, Beal' an Duine. 3. Describe a visit to Stirling Castle.

II. HISTORICAL.

1. Give a brief outline of Stirling's history. 2. Describe the feudal system. 3. Of what did the Scottish armies consist? 4. What can you say of the life of Sir William Wallace? 5. Read Scott's *Marmion* for information about the Battle of Flodden Field.

III. EXPLANATIONS.

1. In your own words give the meaning of the closing stanzas. 2. How do you interpret the "Lay of the Imprisoned Huntsman"? 3. Give meanings of *dark city, buxom, leech, serried, infidel.* 4. Select three figures of speech and explain them.

IV. TO MEMORIZE.

1. Memorize the first stanza of this canto. 2. Make a list of five short passages that should be memorized.

V. FOR ORAL OR WRITTEN COMPOSITION.

1. Write compositions on three of the following topics: (*a*) A Visit to Stirling Castle, (*b*) The Happy Ending of the Poem, (*c*) The View from the Castle, (*d*) Modern Sports in Scotland, (*e*) Ellen in the Guard Room, (*f*) Why I Like *The Lady of the Lake*, (*g*) Why I Do Not Like

The Lady of the Lake, (h) Write a letter to your nearest motion picture manager asking him to show the story of *The Lady of the Lake.*

VI. GENERAL.

1. Debate the following topic in your assembly: Resolved: That Roderick Dhu was a More Worthy Suitor for the Hand of Ellen than Malcolm Graeme. 2. Appoint a member of your class to read *Il Bondocani.* Let him give his narration before the class. Who was the hero of the story? What did he do that was heroic? 3. Compare the introduction to Canto I with the closing stanzas to Canto VI. 4. From your study of this poem what have you learned about the character, interests, and tastes of Sir Walter Scott?

APPENDIX II

JEFFREY'S ANALYSIS OF THE POEM

Edinburgh is proud of the old four-storied house on Charles Street, the birthplace of her gifted son, Francis Jeffrey, who instituted the famous literary magazine, the *Edinburgh Review.* It is needless to remark that Jeffrey and Scott were close friends. From time to time this publisher reviewed for his readers many of Scott's poems and novels, and called attention to the fact that the poet "stands already upon a height to which no other writer has attained in the memory of any one now alive."

For *The Lady of the Lake* Jeffrey had great admiration. The characters and the geographical and historical setting appealed to him, so much that in the *Edinburgh Review* for August, 1810, he gave an analysis of the poem, canto by canto. This analysis is reprinted here.

FIRST CANTO

The First Canto begins with a description of a stag hunt in the Highlands of Perthshire. As the chase lengthens the sportsmen drop off, till at last the foremost horseman is left alone; and his horse, overcome with fatigue, stumbles and dies. The adventurer, climbing up a craggy eminence, discovers Loch Katrine spread out in evening glory before him. The huntsman winds his horn, and sees, to his infinite surprise, a little skiff, guided by a

lovely woman, glide from beneath the trees that overhang the
water, and approach the shore at his feet. Upon the stranger's
approach she pushes the shallop from the shore in alarm. After a
short parley, however, she carries him to a woody island, where
she leads him into a sort of sylvan mansion, rudely constructed
and hung around with trophies of war and the chase. An elderly
lady is introduced at supper; and the stranger, after disclosing
himself to be James Fitz-James, the Knight of Snowdoun, tries
in vain to discover the name and history of the ladies.

SECOND CANTO

The Second Canto opens with a picture of the aged harper,
Allan-bane, sitting on the island beach with the damsel, watching
the skiff which carries the stranger back to land. A conversation
ensues, from which the reader gathers that the lady is a daughter
of the Douglas, who, being exiled by royal displeasure from court,
had accepted this asylum from Sir Roderick Dhu, a Highland
chieftain long outlawed for deeds of blood; that this dark chief is
in love with his fair protégé, but that her affections are engaged to
Malcolm Graeme, a younger and more amiable mountaineer.
The sound of distant music is heard on the lake, and the barges of
Sir Roderick are discovered proceeding in triumph to the island.
Ellen, hearing her father's horn at that instant on the opposite
shore, flies to meet him and Malcolm Graeme, who is received with
cold and stately civility by the lord of the isle. Sir Roderick in-
forms the Douglas that his retreat has been discovered, and that
the king (James V), under pretence of hunting, has assembled a
large force in the neighborhood. He then proposed impetuously
that they should unite their fortunes by his marriage with Ellen,
and rouse the whole Western Highlands. The Douglas, seeing
that his daughter has repugnances which she cannot overcome,
declares that he will retire to a cave in the neighboring mountains
until the issue of the king's threat is seen. The heart of Roderick
is wrung with agony at this rejection; and when Malcolm ad-
vances to Ellen he pushes him violently back, and a scuffle ensues,
which is with difficulty appeased by the giant arm of Douglas.
Malcolm then withdraws in proud resentment, plunges into the
water, and swims over by moonlight to the mainland.

THIRD CANTO

The Third Canto opens with an account of the ceremonies
employed in summoning the clan. This is accomplished by the

consecration of a small wooden cross, which, with its points scorched and dipped in blood, is carried with incredible celerity through the whole territory of the chieftain. The eager fidelity with which this fatal signal is carried on is represented with great spirit. A youth starts from the side of his father's coffin to bear it forward, and, having run his stage, delivers it to a young bridegroom returning from church, who instantly binds his plaid around him, and rushes onward. In the meantime Douglas and his daughter have taken refuge in the mountain cave; and Sir Roderick, passing near their retreat on his way to the muster, hears Ellen's voice singing her evening hymn to the Virgin. He does not obtrude on her devotions, but hurries to the place of rendezvous.

FOURTH CANTO

The Fourth Canto begins with some ceremonies by a wild hermit of the clan, to ascertain the issue of the impending war; and this oracle is obtained — that the party shall prevail which first sheds the blood of its adversary. The scene then shifts to the retreat of the Douglas, where the minstrel is trying to soothe Ellen in her alarm at the disappearance of her father by singing a fairy ballad to her. As the song ends the Knight of Snowdoun suddenly appears before her, declares his love, and urges her to put herself under his protection. Ellen throws herself on his generosity, confesses her attachment to Graeme, and prevails on him to seek his own safety by a speedy retreat from the territory of Roderick Dhu. Before he goes the stranger presents her with a ring, which he says he has received from King James, with a promise to grant any boon asked by the person producing it. As he retreats, his suspicions are excited by the conduct of his guide, and confirmed by the warnings of a mad woman whom they encounter. His false guide discharges an arrow at him, which kills the maniac. The knight slays the murderer; and learning from the expiring victim that her brain has been turned by the cruelty of Sir Roderick Dhu, he vows vengeance. When chilled with the midnight cold and exhausted with fatigue, he suddenly comes upon a chief reposing by a lonely watch-fire; and, being challenged in the name of Roderick Dhu, boldly avows himself his enemy. The clansman, however, disdains to take advantage of a worn-out wanderer; and pledges him safe escort out of Sir Roderick's territory, when he must answer his defiance with his sword. The stranger accepts these chivalrous terms, and the warriors sup and sleep together. This ends the Fourth Canto.

FIFTH CANTO

At dawn the knight and the mountaineer proceed toward the Lowland frontier. A dispute arises concerning the character of Roderick Dhu, and the knight expresses his desire to meet in person and do vengeance upon the predatory chief. "Have then thy wish," answers his guide; and gives a loud whistle. A whole legion of armed men start up from their mountain ambush in the heath; while the chief turns proudly and says, "I am Roderick Dhu." Sir Roderick then by a signal dismisses his men to their concealment. Arrived at his frontier, the chief forces the knight to stand upon his defense. Roderick, after a hard combat, is laid wounded on the ground; Fitz-James, sounding his bugle, brings four squires to his side, and, after giving the wounded chief into their charge, gallops rapidly on toward Stirling. As he ascends the hill to the castle he descries approaching the same place the giant form of Douglas, who has come to deliver himself up to the king in order to save Malcolm Graeme and Sir Roderick from the impending danger. Before entering the castle Douglas is seized with the whim to engage in the holiday sports which are going forward outside; he wins prize after prize, and receives his reward from the hand of the prince, who, however, does not condescend to recognize his former favorite. Roused at last by an insult from one of the royal grooms, Douglas proclaims himself, and is ordered into custody by the king. At this instant a messenger arrives with tidings of an approaching battle between the clan of Roderick Dhu and the king's lieutenant, the Earl of Mar; and is ordered back to prevent the conflict by announcing that both Sir Roderick and Lord Douglas are in the hands of their sovereign.

SIXTH CANTO

The last canto opens in the guard room of the royal castle at Stirling at dawn. While the mercenaries are quarreling and singing at the close of a night of debauch, the sentinels introduce Ellen and the minstrel Allan-bane, who are come in search of Douglas. Ellen awes the ruffian soldiery by her grace and liberality, and is at length conducted to a more seemly waiting place until she may obtain audience with the king. While Allan-bane, in the cell of Sir Roderick, sings to the dying chieftain of the glorious battle which has just been waged by his clansmen against the forces of the Earl of Mar, Ellen, in another part of the palace, hears the voice of Malcolm Graeme lamenting his captivity from an adjoining turret.

Before she recovers from her agitation she is startled by the appearance of Fitz-James, who comes to inform her that the court is assembled, and the king is at leisure to receive her suit. He conducts her to the hall of presence, round which Ellen casts a timed and eager glance for the monarch. But all the glittering figures are uncovered, and James Fitz-James alone wears his cap and plume. The Knight of Snowdoun is the King of Scotland. Struck with awe and terror, Ellen falls speechless at his feet, pointing to the ring, which he has put upon her finger. The prince raises her with eager kindness, declares that her father is forgiven, and bids her ask a boon for some other person. The name of Graeme trembles on her lips, but she cannot trust herself to utter it. The king, in playful vengeance, condemns Malcolm Graeme to fetters, takes a chain of gold from his own neck, and, throwing it over that of the young chief, puts the clasp in the hand of Ellen.

APPENDIX III

TABLE OF SCOTT'S LIFE AND WORKS

1771 Born August 15.
1778 Entered Edinburgh High School.
1785 Entered University of Edinburgh.
1792 Admitted to the Scottish Bar.
1797 Married.
1799 Appointed Sheriff of Selkirkshire.
1802–1803 *Border Minstrelsy.*
1805 *The Lay of the Last Minstrel.*
1806 Appointed "Clerk of Session."
1808 *Marmion.*
1810 *The Lady of the Lake.*
1811 Bought Abbotsford. *The Vision of Don Roderick.*
1812 *Rokeby.* Took possession of Abbotsford.
1813 *The Bride of Triermain.*
1814 *Waverley. The Border Antiquities.*
1815 *The Lord of the Isles. Guy Mannering. The Field of Waterloo.*
1816 *The Antiquary. The Black Dwarf. Old Mortality.*
1817 *Harold the Dauntless.*

1818 *Rob Roy. The Heart of Midlothian.*

1819 *The Bride of Lammermoor. The Legend of Montrose.*

1820 *Ivanhoe. The Monastery. The Abbot.*

1821 *Kenilworth.*

1822 *The Pirate. The Fortunes of Nigel. Peveril of the Peak.*

1823 *Quentin Durward.*

1824 *St. Ronan's Well. Redgauntlet.*

1825 Ballantyne & Co. became bankrupt. *The Betrothed. The Talisman. Tales of the Crusaders.*

1826 *Provincial Antiquities of Scotland. Woodstock.*

1827 *Life of Napoleon Buonaparte. Chronicles of the Canongate,* First Series. (*The Highland Widow. The Two Drovers. The Surgeon's Daughter.*)

1828 *Miscellaneous Prose Works* (six vols.). *Tales of a Grandfather,* First Series. *Chronicles of the Canongate,* Second Series. (*Saint Valentine's Day;* or, *The Fair Maid of Perth.*)

1829 *Tales of a Grandfather,* Second Series. *Anne of Geierstein.*

1830 *Tales of a Grandfather,* Third Series. *The Doom of Devoirgoil: a melodrama.*

1831 *Tales of a Grandfather,* Fourth Series. *Count Robert of Paris. Castle Dangerous.*

1832 Died September 21.

PRONOUNCING VOCABULARY

KEY

ā as in *fate*

å as in *senate*

ă as in *hat*

ä as in *father*

ạ as in *tall*

â as in *care*

ą as in *sofa*

ē as in *we*

ĕ as in *yet*

ė as in *event*

ē as in *her*

ī as in *fine*

ĭ as in *tin*

ō as in *tone*

ŏ as in *hot*

ô as in *orb*

ŏ as in *brother*

o͞o as in *soon*

oͯo as in *foot*

ū as in *tune*

ŭ as in *hut*

û as in *burr*

ụ as in *rule*

ụ as in *full*

ḡ as in *go*

g̣ as in *gem*

ou as in *out*

oi as in *oil*

Allan-bane	ăl' an bān'	Coir-Uriskin	koir ûr' skin
Alpine	ăl' pīn	Coronach	kŏr' ō năk
Ascabart	ăs' cå bärt	Correi	kŏr' ē
Ave Maria	ä' vā ma rē' a	Cushat	kụsh' at
Balvaig	băl vāg'	Devan	dĕv' ån
Bannochar	băn' ŭ kär	Duchray	dū krā'
Battalia	bă tā' lē å	Duncraggan	dŭn crăg'ån
Beala-nambo	bēl' a năm' bō	Dunfermline	dŭn fĕrm' lĭn
Beal' an Duine	bēl' an dụn'		
Beal' maha	bēl' mä hä	Ettrick	ĕt' rĭk
Beltane	bĕl' tān		
Ben-Aan	bĕn ăn'	Ferragus	fēr' a gus
Benharrow	bĕn hâr' rō	Franciscan	frăn sĭs' kån
Ben Ledi	bĕn' lĕd' dē		
Ben-Shie	bĕn' shē	Gael	gā l
Ben Venue	bĕn' vē nụ'	Glenartney	glĕn ärt' ny
Ben Voirlich	bĕn' vôr' lĭk	Glenfinlas	glĕn fĭn' las
Bochastle	bō chăs' le	Glen Fruin	glĕn frū' in
Bothwell	bŏth' wĕl	Glen Luss	glĕn lo͞os
Boune	bo͞on	Graeme	grām
Bracklinn	brăck' lĭn	Guise	gīz
Breadalbane	brĕd' ăl bān		
		Holy-Rood	hŏl y̆ ro͞od
Caledon	kăl' e dŏn		
Cambus	Kăm' bŭs	Idaean	ī dē' ån
Cambusmon	kăm' bŭs mon	Inch-Cailliach	ins kăl' yăk
Cardross	kär'drŏs		
Coilantogle	koil ăn tō' gl	Kernes	kûrns
		Kier	kēr

Lanrick	lăn′ rĭk	Scathe-locke	scăth lŏk
Lendrick	lĕn′ drĭk	Spey	spā
Loch Achray	lŏh ăk rā′	Strath-Ire	străth′ īr′
Lochard	Lŏh ärd′	Strathspey	străth′ spā′
Loch Con	lŏh kon′	Strook	strōōk
Loch Katrine	lŏh kăt′ rĭn	Stumah	stu′ må
Lubnaig	lŭb năg′		
		Taghairm	tăg′ ērm
Maronnan	må rŏn′ ån	Talisman	tăl′ is man
Meggat	mĕg′ åt	Teviot	tĕv′ i ot
Menteith	mĕn tēth′	Tinchell	tĭn′ shell
Monan	mōn′ án	Trossachs	trŏs′ åks
		Truncheon	trŭn′ chon
Naiad	nī′ åd	Tullibardine	tŭl″ i bär′ din
Ochtertyre	ŏk′ ter tīr	Uam-Var	ū′am vär′
Pibroch	pē′ brŏh	Vair	vâr
Prore	prōr	Vaward	vå′ wärd
		Vennachar	vĕn′ nå kär
Rednock	red′ nŏk	Vich Alpine	vĭk ăl′ pīn
Roderick Dhu	rŏd′ er ĭk dụ		
Rowan	rō′ ån	Whinyard	hwĭn′ yärd
Saint Fillan	sänt fĭll′ an	Yarrow	yăr′ rō
Saint Modan	sänt mō′ dn		